ACCOLADES FOR

Gorgeous, brilliantly written, deepl~~...~~ plain stunning. Jamie Blaine is an ~~...~~ writer. His debut is packed with beauty and will blow you away.

—AUGUSTEN BURROUGHS, *NEW YORK TIMES* BESTSELLING AUTHOR OF *RUNNING WITH SCISSORS* AND *THIS IS HOW*

If I had reached the end of my rope, the edge of my hope, and darkness was prevailing. If I stood there on the ledge of lost and losing still—and somehow managed to crawl to some dark barstool corner of the world for one last shot before I gave it all up and caved in, I hope it would be this Jamie and Jesus that walked in behind me. That they pulled up a seat and told me a story and that their telling of it found me right where I was, drowning in this sea called life. And that their story would perform its magic—one funny, dark, raw, honest, loving, wild word at a time, and in so doing, revive my soul. And so they did. This is that book. Read it.

—RIVER JORDAN, BESTSELLING AUTHOR OF *PRAYING FOR STRANGERS*

Jamie Blaine is such an expert at demonstrating the power of the Holy Spirit to work in our lives. *Midnight Jesus* is a collection of stories that show people at their most vulnerable, lonely, and prideful moments when they are crying out for a savior. The Lord works in mysterious ways, and sometimes the most profound truths are looking you right in the eye. There is such a great reward in putting your faith completely in God, knowing that the same God who parted the seas works in our lives today. This is an amazing book that is sure to make an impact on your life.

—MATTHEW BARNETT, COFOUNDER OF THE DREAM CENTER AND SENIOR PASTOR OF ANGELUS TEMPLE

It's so refreshing to see an author with such an honorable background come out of obscurity to share his treasure of experience with the world. Real and rare is what this world deserves, and *Midnight Jesus* by Jamie Blaine packs a powerful punch like no other.

—BRIAN WELCH, LEAD GUITARIST KoRn

Jamie is a mystic of memoirists, a gonzo of evangelists, a Solomon of suffering in the backwaters that too few writers set their sails toward. I find his work arousing for its lyrical beauty and consoling for its gritty wisdom and when I put down his work, I say, with all the meanings of the word converging, man, he's good.

—JOSHUA WOLF SHENK, CREATIVE WRITING INSTRUCTOR AT NYU, AWARD-WINNING AND BESTSELLING AUTHOR OF *LINCOLN'S MELANCHOLY* AND *POWERS OF TWO*

Prophets have nearly always come from the wilderness, raw and a bit angry, to tell us there is more than what we've seen. Jamie Blaine does the same, but he comes from long experience in the wilderness of the human soul and he tells us of the God who dwells there too.

—STEPHEN MANSFIELD, *NEW YORK TIMES* BESTSELLING AUTHOR OF *THE SEARCH FOR GOD AND GUINNESS*

Jamie Blaine articulates a rough faith, peopled with desperate believers, heretics, and in-betweeners—the too far gone and not gone enough, with those who try and fail and fail again. There are no easy answers here, but there is a steady stumbling toward a place where "hoping is more important than knowing." This is a Christianity that could save us from ourselves, and from each other.

—DONNA JOHNSON, AUTHOR OF *HOLY GHOST GIRL* AND WINNER OF THE BOOKS FOR A BETTER LIFE AWARD

With all the hurt and pain in the world today, especially the less desirable roads we find ourselves on, Jamie takes readers on an incredible journey of hope. No matter where you find yourself, read this book to be reminded of the constant truth that every person may experience a new beginning, and that in Christ, beauty can come from the ashes.

—PETE WILSON, SENIOR PASTOR OF CROSS POINT CHURCH AND AUTHOR OF *PLAN B* AND *WHAT KEEPS YOU UP AT NIGHT?*

Jamie's sharp writing takes us into the most intimate and dark moments of these vivid and truer-than-life characters. Super stylized but absolutely authentic, these stories are told visually and with a musicality that punctuates the humor and heartbreak of crisis work and its haunting side effects.

—TONY SHAFF, FILMMAKER/TELEVISION
PRODUCER, MTV NETWORKS

If Saint Paul had written his letters to the guy in the middle row screaming for "Freebird" they would read something like this: a raucous, streetwise, crazy quilt of questioning saints and half-hearted sinners, pumping the jukebox for answers and roller-skating toward redemption, one step ahead of the devil.

—DAVID GIFFELS, WRITER FOR MTV's BEAVIS & BUTTHEAD
AND AUTHOR OF THE HARD WAY ON PURPOSE

If I ever require emergency saving, I definitely want it to come from Jamie Blaine, the coolest dude on fat quad skates. A man filled with genuine empathy, killer licks, and the sense that inspiration is often found in a pair of receding taillights. Deadpan and surprisingly funny, these tales of everyday madness are half Thoreau, half Aquinas, and totally human. Like Raising Arizona for the Bible Belt or deep-Tampa David Lynch. The best and most unlikely book you will buy all year.

—SEAN BEAUDOIN, WRITER FOR THE ONION AND BESTSELLING
AUTHOR OF WISE YOUNG FOOL AND WELCOME THIEVES

In the vein of Don Miller's Blue Like Jazz, Blaine uses everyday interactions to draw closer to the meaning of our existence. Unlike Miller, however, Blaine's interactions are with those who have not only lost their place in society, they have lost their place in the world. With pitch-perfect prose filled with raw heart and humor, Midnight Jesus reveals the hole in all of us that cannot be filled with anything but divine love.

—JOLINA PETERSHEIM, BESTSELLING AUTHOR
OF THE OUTCAST AND THE MIDWIFE

If Christianity has become a stale institution, then Jamie Blaine's *Midnight Jesus* might be the perfect antidote. A raw reminder of the gospel's power.

—PHILIP GULLEY, BESTSELLING AUTHOR
OF *A PLACE CALLED HOPE* AND *FRONT PORCH TALES*

Somewhere between Bukowski and Billy Graham, Blaine packs a spiritual gravity that transcends sect or bias—even for an atheist like me. Sincerely funny, sincerely serious, utterly contemporary, and unexpected. A dangerous, exceptional book.

—JOSH AXELRAD, FORMER PROFESSIONAL BLACKJACK
PLAYER AND AUTHOR OF *REPEAT UNTIL RICH*

Balancing faith and psychology, Blaine comes up with new perspectives on life's biggest questions in a smart and smashingly enjoyable read.

—JOEL MCIVER, BESTSELLING AUTHOR
OF *JUSTICE FOR ALL: THE TRUTH ABOUT
METALLICA* AND *ICE CUBE: ATTITUDE*

Blaine's got the gift that all great storytellers have—the ability to convey the crush of emotions in the tiniest of details. He renders otherwise ordinary people in resplendent detail, painting vignettes in heart-stopping strokes. Jamie is one of a handful of writers who makes me forget that I own a cell phone.

—JOE DALY, *CLASSIC ROCK* MAGAZINE
AND *METAL HAMMER* MAGAZINE

A stupendous achievement. Exhilarating, hilarious, a virtuosic exploration of mental illness in America. Seething with fury and frustration, Blaine captures the reader with great conviction.

—JEFF RAGSDALE, ACTIVIST AND AUTHOR
OF *JEFF, ONE LONELY GUY*

Blaine shares his sharp stories of grit and grace, faith and doubt, humor and heartbreak, details and depth. *Midnight Jesus* is a compelling, hopeful invitation for the reader to pay attention to life, to stay alive to the surprises and the search.

—KENT ANNAN, DIRECTOR OF HAITI PARTNERS AND AUTHOR
OF *FOLLOWING JESUS THROUGH THE EYE OF THE NEEDLE*

Incredibly compelling, at times laugh-out-loud funny collection of short stories.

—BRAD SCHMITT, *THE TENNESSEAN*

A powerful work of creative nonfiction . . . what emerges is the portrait of a man of simple faith, great humor, common doubts and uncommon heart, and readers will likely be glad that Blaine has put his experiences down on paper. They are, quite simply, a revelation.

—*NASHVILLE CITY PAPER*

Blaine mesmerizingly spins tales of love, utter loss, despair, anxiety, uncertainty, hope, and redemption in these reflections of a misfit among misfits.

—*PUBLISHERS WEEKLY*

Blaine writes like a born-again Nick Hornby or Chuck Klosterman. Funny and freewheeling . . . he fails some, rescues many, but listens to them all.

—*SHELF AWARENESS*

MIDNIGHT JESUS

WHERE STRUGGLE, FAITH, AND GRACE COLLIDE

JAMIE BLAINE

THE LATE-NIGHT PSYCHIATRIC CRISIS GUY

W PUBLISHING GROUP

AN IMPRINT OF THOMAS NELSON

Published in Nashville, Tennessee, by W Publishing Group, an imprint of Thomas Nelson.

Author is represented by the literary agency of Alive Communications, Inc., 7680 Goddard Street, Suite 200, Colorado Springs, CO 80920.

Thomas Nelson titles may be purchased in bulk for educational, business, fund-raising, or sales promotional use. For information, please e-mail SpecialMarkets@ThomasNelson.com.

Scripture quotations marked AKJV are taken from the Authorized King James Version. Public Domain.

Scripture quotations marked CEB are taken from the Common English Bible. Copyright © 2011 Common English Bible.

Scripture quotations marked CJB are taken from the Complete Jewish Bible by David H. Stern. Copyright © 1998. All rights reserved. Used by permission of Messianic Jewish Publishers, 6120 Day Long Lane, Clarksville, MD 21029. www.messianicjewish.net.

Scripture quotations marked ESV are taken from the ESV® Bible (The Holy Bible, English Standard Version®). Copyright © 2001 by Crossway, a publishing ministry of Good News Publishers. Used by permission. All rights reserved.

Scripture quotations marked GNT are taken from the Good News Translation in Today's English Version— Second Edition. Copyright © 1992 by American Bible Society. Used by permission.

Scripture quotations marked GW are taken from God's Word®. Copyright © 1995 God's Word to the Nations. Used by permission of Baker Publishing Group. All rights reserved.

Scripture quotations marked ISV are taken from The Holy Bible: International Standard Version. Release 2.0, Build 2015.02.09. Copyright © 1995-2014 by ISV Foundation. All rights reserved internationally. Used by permission of Davidson Press, LLC.

Scripture quotations marked KJV are taken from the King James Version. Public domain.

Scripture quotations marked THE MESSAGE are taken from The Message. Copyright © by Eugene H. Peterson 1993, 1994, 1995, 1996, 2000, 2001, 2002. Used by permission of Tyndale House Publishers, Inc.

Scripture quotations marked NASB are taken from the New American Standard Bible®. Copyright © 1960, 1962, 1963, 1968, 1971, 1972, 1973, 1975, 1977, 1995 by The Lockman Foundation. Used by permission. (www.Lockman.org)

Scripture quotations marked NCV are taken from the New Century Version®. © 2005 by Thomas Nelson. Used by permission. All rights reserved.

Scripture quotations marked NET are taken from the NET Bible®. Copyright © 1996-2006 by Biblical Studies Press, L.L.C. http://netbible.com. All rights reserved.

Scripture quotations marked NIV are taken from the Holy Bible, New International Version®, NIV®. Copyright © 1973, 1978, 1984, 2011 by Biblica, Inc.™ Used by permission of Zondervan. All rights reserved worldwide. www.zondervan.com. The "NIV" and "New International Version" are trademarks registered in the United States Patent and Trademark Office by Biblica, Inc.™

Scripture quotations marked NKJV are taken from the New Kings James Version®. © 1982 by Thomas Nelson. Used by permission. All rights reserved.

Scripture quotations marked NLT are taken from the Holy Bible, New Living Translation. © 1996, 2004, 2007, 2013 by Tyndale House Foundation. Used by permissions of Tyndale House Publishers, Inc., Carol Stream, Illinois 60188. All rights reserved.

Scripture quotations marked TLB are taken from The Living Bible. Copyright © 1971. Used by permission of Tyndale House Publishers, Inc., Carol Stream, Illinois 60188. All rights reserved.

Scripture quotations marked THE VOICE are taken from The Voice™. © 2008 by Ecclesia Bible Society. Used by permission. All rights reserved.

Library of Congress Control Number: 2015908306

ISBN 978-0-7180-3216-6
Printed in the United States of America

1 2 3 4 5 6 RRD 15 16 17 18 19

for the misfits

CONTENTS

CONTENTS

CONTENTS

DISCLAIMER

MIDNIGHT JESUS IS A WORK OF CREATIVE NONFICTION featuring stories from rehab clinics, mental hospitals, church counseling centers, emergency rooms, and correctional facilities. Names, places, faces, and genders have been changed and rearranged in the interest of protecting identities. Any resemblance to persons living or dead is purely coincidental. In some cases, minor story elements have been revised to temper potentially offensive content.

Personally, I don't like footnotes crashing the story and distracting me from the moment at hand. So I added a collection of notes in the back of the book, which contain key scriptures and points of interest.

AUTHOR'S NOTE
Tiny Sparks

NOTHING WILL EVER BE ENTIRELY RIGHT.

Not in this life. I'm just shooting straight here. For most of the people I work with, for many who might read this, life is haphazard at best—one long zigzag path through the mud. Money problems, health problems, self-esteem problems, self-sabotage problems, religion problems, family problems, the complete inability to take five steps in a row without screwing something up.

How do I know this? Because I am some great psychological practitioner of intuition and keen insight? No. Because I am a misfit badly in need of grace and second chances. Because I am moody and incapable and often unsure of anything good. Because even though straight is the way and narrow the path that leads to life, I stumble into the ditches time and again. I am always cutting through the mud.

There are people of faith who somehow find that place where they are standing on the hilltop, smiling and clean in clothes that match, arms lifted in the sun. I am not one of those Christians. I am Peter cursing and falling beneath the waves, Noah fed up and drunk, Thomas doubting, David tiptoeing to get a second peek, Jonah at midnight in the belly of the whale, and Elisha calling down bears. I am mismatched and muddy and ragged, and if there is a hill I'm falling down it backward with both feet in the air.

In other words, I'm one of you. One of us. And even though I know full well that nothing in this life will ever be entirely right, I do believe with all my troubled heart that even with simple grace and the flimsiest, most ramshackle faith, I can keep moving on, pressing on, holding to the good and trusting that there is something more than just this life.

Grace and faith usually have to catch me unaware. They arrive not so much through sermons or lectures or four-point plans, but through stories. No big insights, just little epiphanies— tiny places where the light breaks through. It might be that split second of strange peace in the room of a dying man; one late flash when the addict comes clean; the moment she breathes deep and puts the pistol down; the still, small instant when God walks in; when we are all sons and daughters trying to find our way back home.

This is a book of those snapshot moments. When just for a little while, it feels as if things really could be all right.

INTRODUCTION
Shotgun Jesus and the Empty Spaces

IT'S TWO MINUTES TO MIDNIGHT WHEN THE CRISIS LINE rings.

"Crisis," I answer, fumbling for the phone.

"I've got the pills right here in my hand," she says in a shaky voice. "And if the pills don't do it, I've got a gun. And if I'm too chicken to use the gun, I'll find some other way. 'Cause I just can't go like this anymore."

"Is that really what you want?"

"I don't know what I want anymore," she says. "I just don't know."

"It's your choice," I tell her. "But we can talk about it, if you want."

There's a long silence before she replies. "Yeah," she sighs. "I guess that'd be all right."

"Just tell me where you're at," I say, "and I'll be right there."

I jot down the directions, grab my coat, and head downstairs. "Sorry it's so far," she says, right before I hang up the phone. "Were you sleeping when I called?"

"No ma'am," I reply. "This is what I do. I'm up all night."

IT'S LATE AND I'M DRIVING DOWN A LONG, DARK ROAD thinking about the places I've been. Jesus is riding shotgun. Sometimes he talks and other times he just listens and looks out the side window. Late night in a dark car is a good time to think deep and talk to God about life, the leftover pieces, and all the empty spaces between. About faith, hope, love, and the seemingly broken state of all things. About grace and the lessons learned.

Sometimes I try to sweep the pieces of my life into little piles, thinking some sort of big picture should emerge and things will finally start to make sense. I started out DJing in dive bars and roller rinks, for rock and gospel radio stations. Then it was on to working in mental hospitals and drug rehab centers. I stumbled through college, fumbling my way into a master's degree in counseling psychology. I even took a job as a therapist in a megachurch. For a while, I felt sure I was called to some grand purpose and great adventure. It felt nice to be sure of something. I'm not so sure about a lot of things anymore.

Now I'm the late-night psychiatric crisis guy, driving from jails to bridge rails, backwoods hospitals, and rundown trailer parks in the middle of the night. Meeting people on their worst days, in the worst of places. I don't have enough grace or faith or patience to handle this job on my own, so I made a deal with Jesus that wherever I go, he rides along with me. Because the truth is, most times I don't have a clue what to say or do. Other than show up with Jesus and an attitude of "there but for the grace of God go I," and simply listen to whatever story a person needs to tell.

Everybody's got a story. There are the stories we tell each other, and then there's the truth—the life we live behind the curtain. Jesus knows the story behind the curtain, who we are with the lights out, just where to meet us on the road. That's the Jesus I believe in. I hope and pray that I'm riding with the right, real, one true Jesus, believing the right things. That he meets us on dead-end roads. That grace and mercy can save the day. I hope with all my heart that's true.

THE BIBLE TELLS A LOT OF STORIES. RAMBLING STORIES. Messy stories of messed-up people from Moses to Job, Jonah to John the Revelator. Those stories don't always tie up neatly or resolve. You can't trust a story that's too clean. They taught us that in Psychology 101. True stories are raw and rough, and they don't always end the way we want. But there's a power in unpolished stories when you get down to the true truth—the really real, that rock-bottom honesty with nothing left to lose.

Jesus told stories. And he was reluctant to explain. He left it for the people to make up their own minds.

"Ah, Jesus," I tell him, as he stares out over the fields. "Some things don't ever change."

Left off the highway. Eighteen miles to go. Nothing but starlight and endless fields. There is so much it seems that I will never understand: sin and sickness and the fall of man, why it's just so hard to find one's place. But it's late and I'm driving down a long dark road. Jesus is staring out the side window, quiet now. Seems he's got something on his mind.

PART ONE
ALL THE FALLING STARS

"I will give you treasures from dark,
secret places; then you will know that
I am the Lord and that the God of
Israel has called you by name."

–ISAIAH 45:3 GNT

"All personal theology should begin with
the words: Let me tell you a story."

–SUE MONK KIDD

ONE

JUST START WALKING

"O God, You know my foolishness."

−PSALM 69:5 NKJV

IT'S 6:35 ON A FRIDAY NIGHT AND I'M DRIVING TO WORK AT the roller rink, taking the back way along the levee and the river's edge. There's a certain spot just past the bend on Summer Lane where the road rises and the sun sits on top of the water, sending shimmers of gold across the wake.

Just a little further and my speedometer will flip to a hundred thousand miles. I drive slower, eyes on the gauge's one black nine. At ten miles an hour, the last tumbler creeps by. Sometimes you have to do something ridiculous to mark the seasons of change in life. So I throw the truck in neutral and let it coast. Climb out and walk alongside with one hand holding the open door.

Everything is perspective, so it seems. The sun bleeding into the river, waiting for the nines to turn. Another Friday night, driving to Skate City in my old, beat-up truck. Actually, it's more like a safari wagon than a truck. I just call it a truck. A crack runs across the windshield and the bearings rattle if I go over thirty-five. I looked into getting that fixed, but it was really expensive. So I just try not to go over thirty-five now. It's working pretty well so far.

There's junk littered from back to front: C-plus term papers and old textbooks, and a flannel board laying in the wayback from that first and last time they asked me to teach kids' Sunday school. Laying on top of Jonah's flannel whale, my ex-girlfriend's Abercrombie jacket, left before she dumped me for the youth pastor from a rival church. He's actually a pretty nice guy. Still kinda hurt though.

I guess what they say is true: you really can tell a lot about a person by looking through his car. Fortunes pulled from broken brown cookies, scattered Subway wrappers, and a legion of empty ICEE cups and Diet Coke bottles. An old T-shirt from the bar where I worked before I started going to the Pentecostal church. A stack of CDs on the backseat, topped by Sabbath's *Master of Reality* and a praise and worship collection from that Houston megachurch. I wonder if I'm the only guy in the world walking next to his truck, watching the nines roll by, with heavy metal and gospel CDs side-by-side on the backseat. Probably so.

On the floorboard there's a Cousin Itt bobblehead that my best friend gave me. It's got freakishly long hair, a black hat, and sunglasses. "Reminds me of you," she said. I kept the doll on my dashboard for the longest time, but after she died I broke it from the base and threw it as hard as I could against the windshield. But that just made things sadder, so I fixed it up with some superglue and fastened it to a secret spot beneath the seat. It helps somehow, seeing it there. She loved the river and the stars, radical Jesus and ridiculous things. So I salute the waters and everything beyond the sun, remembering her last words to me: *Jamie baby, just be you.* Easier said, old friend. It seems there's always one thing ending while something else begins.

The shimmers across the river fade to red as the black nine rolls over and the rest give way.

$$100{,}000_n^9$$

I climb back in, shift into first, and pick up the pace a little. Take a left off Summer Lane onto the highway and into the Skate City parking lot. There's a line out front all the way down the walk. I park and slip through the back door, grab a Diet Coke from the fountain, and cue up my first few songs. I charge the smoke machines, enjoying the silence awhile.

"Ready?" asks Mr. Ric, the rink owner, with his hand on the door.

"Ready," I reply.

The front doors open and kids rush in with a racket of laughter, girls dancing and singing along, black lights and cotton candy, arcade games beeping, birthday cakes and disco balls, the smell of hot popcorn and dirty shoes, grape Bubble Yum and junior high perfume.

Skunky Boy skates up fast and barrels over the counter, feet in the air. The kids call him Skunky because he's tanned deep brown from the Southern sun and sports a white-blond fauxhawk. He's making his second pass through fourth grade this year. His mom drops him off with his little sister Lizzy two hours before the rink opens, on her way to wait tables at the Pancake Den.

"Can I borrow a dollar?" he begs, out of breath.

"You mean borrow as in you're gonna pay me back?"

Skunky grins and ducks his head. "Jamie, can I have a dollar?"

"Maybe," I say. "What's it for?"

"If I had another dollar, me and Lizzy could split a Frito Pie," he says, emptying a handful of grimy change onto the counter. "We're starvin'."

"You been digging in the couch cushions?"

"Mama's ashtray," he explains.

I pull out a wadded dollar and iron it straight with my hand. Skunky reaches quick and I anchor it down with my thumb. "Guess who's helping me with trash tonight?"

"Lizzy is?" he replies.

"Who else?"

"Okay, me," he says, raking the fauxhawk tall with his fingers. "I will."

I lift my thumb and he snatches the cash. "Aw, I'da helped you anyway, Jamie," he says. "Even if you didn't give me no dollar."

"Thanks, my man," I tell him. "I'll remember that next time the cans are overflowing with birthday juice."

"Birthday juice?"

"Melted birthday cake," I remind him, "mixed with melted ice cream mixed with a bunch of dumped Fanta Orange."

"Yuck," he says, skating away. "Let Lizzy get that."

"Everybody make a straight line in the middle of the floor," I call out over the mic. "It's limbo time . . ."

I skate out and hang in there for a good five rounds until some little gymnastics brat eliminates me at the third mark from the bottom rung.

"Cheater," I tease, as she takes a victory lap around the limbo stick.

"Loser," she taunts, as I roll back toward the front.

As "Limbo Rock" fades I grab the microphone and speak to the jam-packed crowd. "Keep your food and drinks in the snack bar area at all times," I tell them in my DJ voice. "Skate with the flow, and if you fall down, get up quick as you can. Slow skaters stay to the inside lanes. Are you ready, Skate City?"

I kill the lights and hit the strobes and ten spinning disco balls. Clouds of cherry-red smoke billow from the fog machines in back. "*Are . . . you . . . ready?!*" I repeat. The kids all scream, hands in the air, as another roller-rink Friday night gets under way.

Later, as I clear the floor for the night's first couples' skate, a woman from the moms' section approaches the booth.

"You're gonna need some wheels on your feet if you're coming to ask me to skate," I jibe.

"Not quite," she replies. "But I've been watching you from over there and wanted to ask a question."

"You wanna know if I'll play the Bee Gees?"

"Little before my time," she says. "That's not my question."

"Okay, shoot."

"Are you a college student?"

"Yes ma'am," I answer. "Tryin' to be."

"Ma'am, I like that," she says. "What's your major?"

"Astronomy."

"Really?" she exclaims. "Wow."

"Well, it was," I confess. "But then I switched to English."

7

"English," she nods. "So you want to be a teacher."

"Not even remotely. That's why I changed to biblical archeology."

Her brows knit. She's nodding slower now. "You want to be Indiana Jones?"

"No ma'am, I don't think so. I'm probably about to change again."

She smiles like she gets it now. "You don't know what you want to do."

"I don't have a clue." I fan my arm out over the rink floor. "I mean, come on. Once you've had the most awesomely fun job ever, what else is there?"

"Guess so," she laughs. "Does roller rink DJing pay the bills?"

"Not quite."

"I'm director out at Forest Hills Psychiatric Facility," she says, passing me her card. "You seem pretty good with people, kids and all. I'm looking to hire a new night tech. It's a great little college job."

"Psychiatric," I reply. "Is it dangerous?"

"No more dangerous than skating," she says. "Probably."

"Okay, maybe," I tell her. "You need me to fill out an application or something?"

"I think I know what I need to know," she says, heading back to the moms' table at the snack bar's edge. "If you're interested, come see me next week."

"Sure you don't wanna hear the Bee Gees?" I call.

"Why not?" she replies. "Everybody loves the Bee Gees."

Gymnastic Brat and Skunky Boy skate up and knock on my glass. "Uh, Jamie?" Brat snaps, in a tone way too smart for a seven-year-old. "Where's my dollar, huh?" She taps her foot, holding out her hand.

Skunky offers a clueless smile, chili all over his face. I sigh and turn my pockets inside out. "Last one, girl," I tell her. "DJ broke."

"Ugh," she grunts, disgusted. "Maybe DJ need a real job."

SUNDAY MORNING AT THE PENTECOSTAL CHURCH. SWEATY men in flashy suits jump pews while big women swoon, sprawled out in the aisles and covered by shawls with Bible verses embroidered at the fringes in silver and blue. The congregation sways, singing seven-word songs, eleven minutes long. Holy Rollers have the best music by far, that electric mix of country, soul, and rock and roll, slain in the Spirit and Jericho march.

Pastor Reddy paces the pulpit, preaching fire so hot the people fan themselves with the programs. Then he takes us to the mercy seat with tears streaming down his face. He circles round again, higher, faster, louder, until at last the congregation collapses at the altar begging for second chances to start again. Chaos and ecstasy, laughter and tears, shouts in tongues and hallelujahs. Sweet Jesus, earthy and concerned and always so very close.

What am I doing here? I do not really know. I grew up Catholic and was Southern Baptist for a while. I spent a season in agnostic curiosity after things fell apart. Maybe it's the music or the emotion or the spectacle of it all. Maybe it's nice for church not to be so robotic and dull. Maybe I'm looking for something too. Sure, some of these people are flaky, and a lot of them are just plain nuts. But the ones who are genuine have a joy and peace that is truly unique. For that alone, it's worth checking out.

Pastor Reddy had a preaching program on Saturday afternoons back at the gospel radio station where I DJed, and sometimes we'd hang out and talk after the show was done. He seemed pretty easygoing off the mic, a decent enough guy. I told him I worked days on Christian radio and DJed in bars at night. I didn't see any problem with it. To Reddy's credit, he never criticized or pushed. He seemed sincerely interested in me, asking questions and listening to what I had to say. When he invited me to church, I showed up and liked it enough to keep coming back.

The Christian station fired all the DJs and switched to sports talk. For me it was the bar on Saturday nights and Sunday morning church for a while. Then I started playing guitar and singing for a gospel band. Next thing I knew they were asking me to speak at a few church functions here and there and help with the youth. That's when I quit the bar. I figured it was the right thing to do.

Truth is, sometimes I'm torn. We probably need more church folks who work in bars. On slow nights I would bartend, and I enjoyed taking care of people, listening to their stories, and putting them in cabs when they were too far gone. Apparently Jesus spent a lot of time in bars, so there's gotta be some message there. Jesus also really upset a lot of church people. Sometimes it's hard to know the right thing to do. That's why I catch Pastor Reddy in the foyer after service to see what he thinks about taking a job at the psych ward. A second opinion never hurts.

"Psych ward?" he asks. "Doing what?"

"Don't know, really," I tell him. "Just working with people and stuff, I guess."

Reddy has this habit. He looks you straight in the eye then he half-smiles and looks all around you like he's checking out your aura or something. Then he'll speak.

"I feel a peace about it, little brother," he says. "You can help teach people about Jesus. God could use you to change a person's heart."

"Really?" I reply. "You think?"

The preacher smiles bigger now, with no direct reply. He stoops in and loops his arm around me from the side. "God rarely gives specifics," he tells me. "He says, 'Just start walking and I'll show you the way.'"

"Start walking," I repeat.

"Yep," Reddy says. "That's how you find the way."

TWO

THIS IS NOT TV

"Lord, you tricked me."

—JEREMIAH 20:7 NCV

FOREST HILLS IS A PSYCHIATRIC WARD LOCATED OUT PAST the mill in a small Southern town, a catchall for addicts, schizophrenics, people too depressed to function, bipolar housewives, obsessive-compulsive cutters, anorexic beauty queens, and sullen, wayward teens. It's a sprawling estate with a long, narrow drive that cuts back off the main road. The central hospital looks like a big, brick rancher from the front, but individual units stretch far back into the pines. There are horses and a swimming pool and a full-sized gym.

Great job for a college kid. Psych techs get free meals, use of the laundry, time to study. Every night there're movies and dominoes and volleyball. Punctuated by patients screaming profanities, occasional naked anarchy, and free-for-all psychotic wrestling matches.

Straitjackets have recently been banned, labeled inhumane, so when something breaks loose, it's up to the techs to lock it down with physical restraints. I know a few holds from buddies in the wrestling business, and an old cowboy bouncer taught me this secret: Be kind, keep your cool, make it your goal that no one gets hurt, and things will almost always end well. Other than the occasional carpet burn, he's right.

IT'S MY FIRST NIGHT AFTER ORIENTATION. I'M WORKING ON my own. There's a rush of static before the announcement breaks over the psych ward PA system.

"Dr. Strong, PICU."

There are four main units at Forest Hills Psych: (1) Adult, (2) Addiction ADU, (3) Adolescent, and (4) Acute PICU: Psychiatric Intensive Care Unit, a superlockdown for severely violent or psychotic patients.

"*Dr. Strong, PICU!*"

Code Blue calls for resuscitation. Code Red is for fire. Code Black for severe weather. Dr. Strong means a combative patient or assault—all staff arrive *stat*.

I sprint down the long hall from adolescent, past addiction, and take a right through the adult unit. There's a narrow pane in the PICU door. Through it I see a giant man with savage eyes, wearing white pajamas with big green stripes. He shouts, "*Die Devils!*" and heaves an end table into the Plexiglas.

"*DR. STRONG, PICU!*"

Jackie, the RN, has barricaded herself in the nurses' station. She bugs out her eyes and waves me in. I turn and scan the east hall. The west. The wall clock reads 1:13 a.m. No one else is coming. Green Stripes growls about Uncle Sam's cameras and kicks through the wall. The nurse has spotted me; it's too late to slip away. The patient turns, his arms and chest puffed out; we stare at each other through the pane. He's a lot bigger than me. Older and slower maybe, but infused with the power of psychosis. *Help*, I pray, paralyzed but too curious to turn away. The acid smell of adrenaline is in the air. No one else is coming. I fumble for my key and open the door.

"Easy," I tell him as I ease into the room. "Easy." His snake eyes follow me, flickering red as he picks up a nearby chair and holds it high by the legs.

I grab a chair, too, and we circle each other like gladiators.

Why did I grab that chair? Because it's like I'm watching this on TV. Yet it feels like I'm on TV too. So if this were a movie, what would I do next?

Swing first, my senses tell me. *He's huge.*

"Don't hurt him, Jamie," Jackie wheezes, calmer now. "We don't need no more lawsuits."

Nobody gets hurt, I pray again. *This is not TV.*

We lock eyes with chairs up, waiting. "Go on, kill me, Mole Man," Green Stripes cries. "You been wantin' to long enough."

"No, brother," I tell him. "I'm just here to help."

His shoulders slump; he looks confused. "All I wanna do is go home," he says.

"I wanna go home too," I reply. Green Stripes lowers his chair to the floor. I drop mine to the side, breathe for what seems like the first time in ages, and try to stop shaking.

"Come on," I tell him. "Patient next door went AWOL and left a whole pack of Camels behind. Let's go outside."

The night is so black we're just shadows in the courtyard. It's too dark to see anything but the other's shape. We sit for the longest time, neither of us speaking—the calm that comes after chaos.

"Sometimes," he says, "my mind plays tricks on me."

"Yeah," I tell him. "Mine too."

The back lounge window is open and Jackie's in the med room humming that old song about Spanish angels at the altar of the sun. A jet streams over, wing lights softly blinking. For a long time we watch it climb.

"But one day," he says, eyes lifted. "I'll be free."

"One day," I repeat.

We follow the lights as they flicker across the sky, silent until the airplane vanishes from sight.

"Jamie," Jackie calls, peering through the screen. "Y'all okay?"

"Yes ma'am," I reply. "We are now."

THREE

THERE BUT FOR THE GRACE

*"Jesus was not crucified in a cathedral
between two candles, but on a cross between
two thieves ... at the kind of place where
cynics talk smut, and thieves curse, and
soldiers gamble. Because that is where He
died. And that is what He died about."*

–GEORGE MACLEOD

FOREST HILLS ADDED A PREADOLESCENT UNIT. ON THE second day it's open, a nine-year-old pyromaniac sets fire to the curtains by packing a microwave with aluminum foil and setting the timer to 9:99. Smoke fills the ward; Jackie passes out. We're short staffed again. An alcoholic Klansman from the rehab wing breaks through the side door and helps me evacuate the kids.

Firemen arrive as the drapes smolder. The Klansman stands in the courtyard with a tiny black girl in his arms. The preadolescent unit closes the very next day.

AN ELEMENTARY SCHOOL PRINCIPAL SNEAKS OUT OF VISitation, shucks off her clothes, and dashes into traffic stark naked. A schizoaffective meth freak mods his Honda so he can refill the gas tank from cans stacked on the passenger side, while driving. By the time state troopers catch him, he's already logged over eighteen hundred miles nonstop. A schizoaffective astrophysicist draws me a fairly coherent diagram of how to build an elevator to the moon.

FOR FRIDAY'S COMMUNITY GROUP, I BRING IN MY GUITAR and take requests. I quite possibly might be the only psych tech ever to play "Back in Black" back to back with "Jesus Loves Me." But somehow, it works. The girl in bed sixteen sweet-talks me into lending her my pen and promptly stabs her roommate. A former patient who once won an Elvis impersonator contest at the county fair sees me at the Piggly Wiggly and chases me down aisle nine with a family-sized can of pork and beans.

"Long-hair sumbitz!" he yells as I dash past produce. "Try'n lock me up again!"

I'M WATCHING A MOVIE WITH THE PATIENTS WHEN SMILEY– the seventy-four-year-old, flame-haired charge nurse who still mows her grass in a bikini—sends me to retrieve a new admit from the front door. I make my way up and find myself face-to-face with an actress from the very same film.

"Can you, uh, hang on a second?" I ask her, trying to figure out just how to tactfully bring her back. "Wait right here."

Later that night, America's foremost authority on ancient aliens punches me in the back of the head and accuses me of stealing his Cheetos.

THE PSYCH WARD CAN BE A LITTLE ABSURD SOMETIMES. Scary. Funny. Sad. I wouldn't call it a depressing place, though. Depressing is some cubicle farm or corporate office. The smell of copy toner and desperate coffee. But a table full of old drunks and delirious misfits playing *Monopoly*, laughing and talking about the stuff in life that matters? That's not depressing. That's rich and real and true.

There's something strangely hopeful about badly broken people coming together to try and find their way through the ugliest parts of life. If there's hope in the darkest parts, you have to figure that maybe hope is going to win in the end. That hope just might be stronger than despair. When you see people walk through the worst and come out on the other side, it makes you hopeful too. There's a lot of grace and humor in psych wards. Has to be.

Still, it's not like the mental hospital is one long Hallmark movie of never-ending fairytale epiphanies. Some nights it's just plain bizarre.

I TAKE FOUR PARANOID SCHIZOPHRENICS AND A DELU-
sional nymphomaniac bowling. There's a Knights of Columbus
group in the next lane over. We intermingle, joking around, having a big time. "You guys are crazy!" a KOC woman with a tag
that says

HELLO, MY NAME IS FLORENCE exclaims. I am bound
to confidentiality as to who we are or where we are from. So I let
it ride.

Stanley, the most reasonable of our bunch, leans in to me and
whispers with the most pleasant smile, "Jamie, that witch calls
me crazy again and I'll crack her head open with this twelve-
pound ball."

"Hey guys?" I call to my group. "Time to go. Let's ride."

A THIRTY-SIX-YEAR-OLD MOTHER OF TWO ESCAPES THE
psych ward, tracks down a member of my family, and convinces
them we are long-lost friends. I find her on my doorstep in a
sheer, pink gown with her clothes in a Barbie backpack.

"I left everything for you," she sings, off-key seductively. "We
were meant to be."

A TEENAGE BOY MAKES A NOOSE WITH TWO TOWELS AND
the shower curtain rod. The house painter from the adult unit
jumps off the roof. A sixty-five-year-old woman ties a trash bag
around her head. The son of a millionaire smashes his car into
a bridge. They all survive and somehow find a way to carry on.

"Small steps," the teen boy tells me while holding the old
woman's hand. "One at a time."

IT'S AN EXPLICITLY DISASTROUS NIGHT OF DOUBLE TAKE-downs, psychotic breaks, multiple admits, escape attempts, and copycat episodes of self-harm. We somehow manage to get everyone calmed down, medicated, and into bed. Slipping out to the rehab patio, I find a retired Episcopal priest smoking his pipe and studying the twelve steps. I flop down in the rocker beside him. "All right, Father," I ask. "Got any advice for me on this helping people thing?"

He looks me over, lighting his pipe again. "You have to go empty, son," he says. "With no agenda. Never think you're above it all. You show up like someone who barely escaped the fire, found water, and returned to rescue those who are left."

"No agenda," I reply.

The old priest pulls a slimline Bible from his pocket and flips through pages until he finds his place. "In returning and rest, you will be saved," he reads. "In silence and trust you shall find your strength."

I nod along, rock awhile. *What's that supposed to mean?* "Anything else?"

His grey eyes sparkle as he fills the air with the glorious smell of Captain Black. "Find the secret place," he says. "And let God give you rest."

A DESPONDENT STAY-AT-HOME MOM BREAKS THE BLADE from a razor, carves into her wrist, and writes *The wages of sin is death* in blood across her bathroom wall. An addict tries to get high on coffee creamer. The sweet, mild-mannered girl in room twenty-two is caught running an inpatient prostitution ring. An NBA star offers me five hundred dollars to bring him some weed.

SOMETIMES IT SIMPLY BREAKS YOU TO SEE SO MANY wrecked lives. Scratch below the surface and you'll find crossed wires and good intentions, people trying to do the best they can. Messed-up chemistry, messed-up family, chain-reaction catastrophes crushing the will to live. These are not unbelievers. These are people who work and pray and believe with all their hearts. Someone's sister or mother or daughter or friend. There's no such thing as *those people*. Those people are us. Me and you. And quite honestly, that's harder to deal with sometimes.

WHEN A LEGAL CRISIS THREATENS TO CLOSE OUR DOORS, Smiley sends me to fetch the head psychiatrist from a honky-tonk out past the city-limit sign. When I find him he's three sheets to the wind, two-stepping with some leathery Jezebel in spandex pants while the country-and-western band sizzles through their own smokin' cover of "Brick House."

"Doc!" I yell over blistering fiddle and steel, yanking at the tassels of his cowboy jacket. "You gotta come with me or they're gonna shut us down."

"All right, Jamie. I'll go," he boozily concurs. "But you gotta dance with Judy first."

"Ooh," Judy coos, "I remember you." The air is smoky and lights dim. But I remember Judy too. Former patient. Addiction unit.

"Ma'am," I tell her, straight as George Strait. "I cain't dance."

She looks me up, then down again, the way a long-haul trucker stares at a country-ham-and-grits buffet. "Sugar britches," she says, right eye twitching when she smiles. "I can sure show you how."

HOARDERS AND VOYEURS AND THE GIRLS WITH PICA DIAG-noses who eat paper and glass. Dissociative fugues and rages and kleptos and agoraphobes. Winos, pillheads, coke fiends, speed freaks, and people who lost their houses to the dollar slot machines. Sometimes I think, *There but for the grace of God go I.* Other times it's like, *Not me. Never in a million years.*

I go from one or two shifts a week to working nearly every night. It is the most difficult, exhilarating, fascinating, frustrating, tragic, comedic job I have ever had. Aside from the times it drives me nuts, I truly love it. So much, in fact, that I change my major to psychology.

"Oh, Jamie," Liza, the lead therapist on the adult unit, replies, "tell me you didn't, please."

CHRISTMAS NIGHT. ONLY ELEVEN PATIENTS REMAIN ON the ward—the ones without a pass or family nearby. Everyone mopes, shut up in their rooms. I announce there's a mandatory AA meeting at a church out by the college.

"For everybody," I insist. "Even if you don't drink."

Grumbling, the patients load into the van and we drive across town. The heater in the church basement is broken, so we leave our coats on and huddle close. It's a small and desperate meeting, but the spirit is strong.

Afterward, I take the van down Christmas Card Lane over in the nice part of town. The streets are teeming. People abandon their cars, walking the lane to gawk at swanky estates draped in a plethora of twinkly lights and giant blow-up sleds. Santa passes out hot chocolate as Frosty dances with the kids. There's a forty-foot cross on the highest hill, and a crowd is gathered there. We stand in their midst with hands joined, everyone singing "Silent Night."

There's a junkie on my left and a patient with numerous failed suicides holding on to the right. "God Bless, Jamie," the junkie says. "This is what it's all about."

FOUR

MONK BY DEFAULT

*"Jesus was asked 183 questions. He only
directly answered three. But he asked 307."*

−MARTIN COPENHAVER

THIRD-FLOOR CLASSROOM, LAST SEAT ON THE RIGHT BY
the window. On the sandy banks below, that cute but brutal
troop of Amazons known as the girls' college volleyball team
practices as Dr. Figgpen lectures about futility and man's long
search for meaning.

"Suffering is like a gas," Figgpen says, just as a redhead with
seven-foot legs flies high and slams the ball into her opponent's
face. "And just like the properties of gas, suffering completely
fills the human soul and mind."

Redhead's rival is a squat brunette with granite thighs. The
ball ricochets high off her head. She shakes off the smash, dives,
and bunts it back for the score. The redhead ducks the net and
helps her adversary from the sand. She stands and the two high-
five, embrace quickly, and return to opposite sides.

"Therefore the size of suffering is relative," Figgpen continues. "It's incorrect to assume that a man who loses one leg suffers only half that of a person who loses both. It is only correct to say both suffer. Suffering consumes all."

Psychology is deep waters. At church we obsess over the answers; in theories of psych class, it seems all we talk about is the questions. Sometimes I feel caught between trying to shake hands with both sides, my arms too short to span the gap.

Why does the evidence seem to show that humans are not hardwired for delayed reward? How does that work with the "store up your treasures in heaven" plan in the Bible? Is that why we keep screwing up and falling off the wagon? Why, despite incredible advances in technology, we're still struggling with the same basic spiritual and philosophical issues we had six thousand years ago? Why are we so attuned to the faults of others, yet blind to our own? Were we simply created to fail? And if evolution's your thing, why are we still so socially and mentally stuck? Shouldn't we have advanced past the need for rescue by now?

So much of our fate depends on variables beyond our control—chemistry, genetics, the conditions we faced in formative years. Some rise above the worst while others fall despite the most favorable of circumstances. What inspires one, crushes another. It's enough to boggle your mind.

Why do good times pass quickly while difficult times drag by? Shouldn't it be the other way around? Why is death so painful and sad? Wouldn't it help with matters of belief if death were one last season of euphoria and joy?

Here's another bomb the prof drops on us: "One day you'll long for the things you take for granted now. Even the struggles."

Well, great. This is why the French invented profanity. Let

me get this straight: humans are largely incapable of appreciating goodness until it's too late? Doomed to want mostly what we don't have, until we lose it? And someday we'll even miss the parts that seem difficult now? That seems wrecked.

So what's the cure? Can religion help us rise above the frustrating truths of life? Or does it just put pressure on us to be less than real? Or is that what true religion is? The fight against futility? The struggle to keep hope alive?

Why are we discussing life's deepest questions in psychology class instead of church? No wonder my preacher seemed a little freaked out when I told him I changed my major to psych. This is dangerous stuff.

Church speaks of the power of faith and prayer; in psychology class we discuss the importance of choice and responsibility. There's truth in balance. But that's the hard part. The balance. Faith isn't magic. Faith is the weight. Faith and work go hand in hand.

Is God in charge? Or did God leave us in charge? Is there a way for both statements to be true? I'm not trying to be blasphemous or cynical or critical; these are important questions. And even if we never find satisfactory answers, isn't it worth the pursuit?

I tune out and turn back to the window just in time to see the girls' squad scamper off the sand as the boys' team takes their place. Some dude who looks like a cross between Gilligan and Tom Cruise sets up a two-man spike. His teammate soars and slams the ball into the sand on the other side. They nod, adjust their sunglasses, and slap each other's behinds.

"Well, so much for man's search for meaning," Dr. Figgpen says, closing the textbook and walking between the seats to wake up dreamers like me. "Let's move on to something a little more concrete . . ."

Figgpen finds an empty desk, perches on top with legs crossed, and begins the tale of an old monk who talked about freedom through self-control, holy living by learning to watch and be still. Walking lightly through this life as a stranger, a shape-shifter, quick to laugh and slow to speak. Do less, be less. Master the early exit. Disappear and find the seams. Because that's where you find the face of God, the old monk says. In the seams.

The campus spreads out beyond the sandy banks. Cleveland Library towers over the water, a cascade fountain in the quad. Hudson Hall sits down on the shore of the cypress grove. I lived a lifetime's worth of memories there last year. We kept a johnboat tied just outside our dorm room door and would troll the river at night, feeding ducks at the footbridge, singing to the coeds as they walked across the way. Sneaking into the stadium after the lights went down, piling into cars for midnight runs.

Every day was a new adventure, a whirlwind of exciting people and plans and feeling like I had life's path mapped out. I was one of the most popular kids on campus. Then it all went off the rails. Like my magnets flipped backward and suddenly, instead of attracting, I was pushing everyone away. Like some strange rapture where everybody just left me behind.

What happened? I'm still not sure. People you think will be lifelong companions simply drift away, move on, or find an off-ramp, their own right place to be. Now my social life consists mostly of the psych ward and skating rink. Schizophrenics and sixth graders. Wonder what that means? They say you get into psychology trying to figure out your own life. Maybe that's true. All I know is, these days, I spend a lot of time trying to find the seams.

Stranger, shape-shifter. Monk by default, guess that's me.

FIVE

GOTTA RUN TO KEEP FROM HIDING

"All you have to do is listen."

–LESTER BANGS

THE HOSPITAL OFFERS ME A SLOT ON INTAKE AND ASSESSment. Three nights a week, from six at night until six in the morning, I'm on standby for crisis calls and on-site evaluations.

Florentine is the intake manager. With his trim mustache and black helmet of hair, he looks like a tough but smart-aleck detective from an eighties cop drama. "Most things you can handle over the phone," he says. "But if you have to go out and get stuck, call me. You know how to take vital signs, right?"

"Yeah, sure," I tell him. "Why?"

"Lot of alcoholics try to show up cold turkey. If you get somebody going into withdrawals," he says, "stop at the liquor store and get 'em a drink. You don't want nobody dying on your watch."

"I'll call you," I reply.

"Just act like you know what you're doing," Florentine suggests, "and nobody will ever know."

They pay me fifteen dollars an hour to go out on a call, two bucks an hour just to standby. A month of free money passes before my first dispatch at ten after ten on an icy Thursday night.

The caller says the patient has been a closet binge drinker for a long time. There was a dramatic intervention and the family wants him in rehab—tonight.

"We're counting on you, sir," the caller says. "It's pretty near life-or-death at this point."

A fallen angel from the psych ward once told me that if I ever felt scared or insecure, to just become someone else.

"Like an actor," she said.

I pull on my lambskin coat and black cowboy hat and set out to meet the patient at the far end of the Rite Aid parking lot.

The green Camry the caller described waits, idling. I park at the Quik Stop down the street and sit for what feels like a long time, staring at the car. *God,* I pray. *A little help here for the Midnight Rider or I'll mess this up real bad . . .*

Gathering my act, I walk across the lot and look down through the car window at my grandmother's next-door neighbor. Friendly guy, blue-collar, gentle with his wife and kids. I start to tell him I stopped at the store for some Funyuns and a Diet Coke and happened to see him there.

"Oh no," he moans. "It's you."

"Chris," I say. "This ain't your car."

"My brother-in-law's," he says. "Guy that called. I didn't want nobody to come with me. I haven't been drinking today. Been trying to straighten up but it's . . ." His forehead drops to the steering wheel and he starts to sob, cursing and punching the dash.

I look down the street toward my truck. It's too late to leave. I don't know what to do.

"Hey, brother," I say, hunching down, elbows on the doorframe. "It'll be all right. I'm gonna get you to a better place."

"You don't know how bad it is."

I go around and climb in on the passenger side. "Trust me. Been doing this stuff a long time. You're here now. You made the right choice. Things can be okay." These words, I don't even know where they come from.

"Nothin's ever been okay," Chris says. He turns to me and holds out a trembling hand. His fingernails are caked with grease from a part-time job at Eastside Tire and there's a purple welt beneath his eye. "I'm broke. My wife's ready to leave me. I tried to quit a thousand times. But I can't, man. I just can't."

"If you're ready, I'll get you in," I say. "But you gotta want it. It's up to you."

Chris nods like he knows what I'm saying is true. He leans against the wheel. We sit in the sounds of passing traffic and the low hum of yellow streetlights. The car smells like old books and Armor All. There's dog hair on the seats. The emotion dies down a bit.

"So what's with the getup?" he asks.

"This is my first real call," I confess. "And this lady at the psych ward said if I was nervous to become somebody else, like in a movie or something."

"Really?" he says.

"Really," I reply.

"Counselor told you this?"

"No. A patient."

"And this is where you're gonna send me?"

"Pretty much, yeah."

Chris sits back in the seat and rolls his head from side to side. Even though it's cold and his window is open, sweat runs in rivulets down his face.

"I don't know. I don't know if I can make it tonight."

"Let's just take it one step at a time," I say, eyeing the neon Bacardi sign in the Rite Aid window. "First, let me check your pulse." I press my fingers to his wrist for fifteen seconds. "One thirty-two," I tell him. "How do you feel?"

"Like hell."

"Dude, you're in detox. Let's go in the store, I'll buy you whatever you want to drink."

Chris ducks down and studies the signs. Starts to speak but pulls back. "No," he says, handing me the keys. "If we're going, let's go right now."

I'm driving the Camry toward rehab, figuring I've got a good excuse for barreling down the expressway with the needle on ninety-five. Chris has the passenger seat laid all the way back and his arm over his eyes.

"Blaine," he grunts as we near the exit.

"Yeah?" I say.

"I'm glad it was you."

SIX

OCEANS OF GRACE

"I'm after mercy, not religion."

–JESUS, MATTHEW 9:12–13 MSG

A PREACHER NAMED PONDER COMES ON SUNDAY NIGHTS to do psych-ward church in the dining hall. I let him in and we go to fetch the podium from the kitchen closet when Big Mike, a soon-to-be graduate from the rehab wing, passes back through from a family visit.

"Hey Jamie," Big Mike says, walking over to where we stand. "You takin' us to play volleyball tonight?"

"Sure, probably," I tell him.

"You oughta see this effin' guy," he says to Ponder. "He'll jump ten foot high and hit a backcourt slam outta nowhere and you'll be like, *That lil' son-of-a—*"

"Mike, this is Brother Ponder. He preaches the church service here."

"Aw, Reverend," Big Mike says, dragging his hand down his face. "Sorry 'bout that."

"Tell you what," Ponder laughs. "Come to church tonight and I'll let it slide. Gonna be a good one. I'm preaching on grace."

"Deal," says Mike. "I probably need it."

Ponder preaches on grace every time. He'll tell the old stories of how he'd drank enough Brut aftershave to float a battleship, how when he couldn't get Brut he'd strain shoe polish through a sock, how he'd been married three times and shot twice, locked up in seven states and tried to kill himself with ropes, razors, guns, and pills and never could succeed. Ponder's got the right testimony for psych-ward church.

"Bring me a big crowd tonight, Jamie," he asks. "It's gonna be good. I can feel it."

At a quarter to six I go from hall to hall. Anyone who wants to go to church can go. Some attend because they're desperate; others just go to get off the unit for a while. Wayne is a tiny Irishman with Tourette's and ADD. He falls into the group with Darrell, who's been diagnosed as a bipolar, paranoid schizophrenic, manic-depressive, sex, and crystal-meth addict with intermittent explosive disorder. We get a lot of those. Ponder seems pleased when I bring him twenty-two patients in all.

"Bless you, Brother Jamie," he says. I nod and take a seat in the back of the room.

Ponder goes into his spiel about drinking oceans of aftershave and sleeping in barrels beneath the bridge. About one woman who cut him and another who stole his car.

"Big boobs!"

It's Wayne, of course. He'll do all right for a while, rocking and staring intently, and then something inappropriate will burst loose. The idiot tech on Friday night decided to let some of the patients watch *Showgirls,* and it hasn't helped Wayne's condition one bit. A few patients laugh but Ponder keeps steady and starts in on his redemption, the old Asian woman who fed him from the café backdoor, who bandaged his wounds and showed him the love of—

"Did you know the pope is the Antichrist?" Darrell is standing now, holding up his hand.

"Brother, I'm not Catholic," Ponder politely says. "Can we talk after service?"

"Oh," says Darrell, returning to his seat. "Okay."

I motion Ponder on. He continues about the Asian lady who showed him the love of God through her actions when he was a dirty street bum who only weighed a hundred and ten pounds, how her family took him in and got him clean and sober and—

"Big ol' big knockers!" Wayne barks.

Giggles and muffled laughs across the room. Ponder stops now. I move up and sit in the chair next to Wayne. Like that's going to help. He folds his arms down on the table and rests his head on top. I lay my hand against his back as Ponder clears his throat and soldiers on.

He preaches now about the church that accepted him as is, how he struggled with temptations as God began to change his heart. How the church people encouraged him and sometimes would slip bills into his hands and pockets. One time he even found a hundred—

"Six six six is on the hundred-dollar bill," Darrell announces with concern. "If you got one, I can show you."

Big Mike pounds the table and stands. "Will you shut your mouth and let the freakin' preacher preach?"

Ponder steps away from the podium and clasps his hands behind his back.

I've got Darrell's sleeve now, waving Big Mike down. "Mr. Darrell, you got to be calm or you can't stay, okay?"

"But Jamie," he cries, "if I don't warn these people . . . who will?" Darrell says it so sincerely that I consider asking Ponder if he'll let him have the mic for a while.

"Darrell, buddy," I tell him, hand on his shoulder, "Maybe you better head back."

"I'll be quiet, I promise," he pouts. "Let me sit in the back with you."

As we head to the rear of the room, Ponder picks right back up on his prodigal road home.

"But the Lord's hand was upon me, guiding me through the night like the North Star—"

"Big boobs Christmas!"

I collar Wayne and bring him along. We sit there by the back windows, one on each side of me, Wayne rocking back and forth and occasionally jerking and biting the sleeve of his coat, Darrell murmuring about King Juan Carlos and the barcode mark of the beast.

Ponder walks around to the front of the podium. "Every day I struggle," he tells us. "I've cussed and fought and my own mind has betrayed me so many times. Every day I try to find some-place to belong and be all right. Some days I do, some I don't. But I believe the good news is that Jesus loves the people nobody else will. Jesus meets us and loves us just like we are."

The room is quiet now. Darrell and Wayne are still.

"And I believe he's right here with us tonight, right here in this hospital dining room, ready with acceptance and love and grace. Some of you might say, 'Brother Ponder, you don't know where I've been, you don't know the things I've done.' Jesus knows and he says, 'Come on, I'll take you.' He says 'I love you anyway, just like you are.'"

Ponder lets his words linger. The dining room is dark except for a few stray lamps and streetlights bleeding in from the big picture window. The smell of biscuit dough hangs heavy in the air.

"If there's anything you need to talk about, anything you want prayer for, come on down front and we'll all go to God together, just as we are."

All twenty-two patients rise and meet Brother Ponder down front. It's a moment so real and true it makes me want to take off my shoes. For a little while, the old cafeteria feels like holy ground.

In a nod to Billy Graham, Ponder points back to me and asks, "The buses will wait, brother?"

"The buses will wait," I reply.

After the service, Ponder walks back with us to the unit door. I corral my people inside, the preacher shaking hands with them as they file through. Wayne gives Ponder a hug and Darrell says, "You're coming back next week, right?"

"Next week and the week after," the preacher says. "God willing, every Sunday til I die."

"Okay," says Wayne. "I'll be here too."

As the last person passes, Ponder reaches through and grabs my sleeve. "I do believe that's about the best service we've ever had."

"You said it'd be good," I tell him. "Sorry about all the yelling and stuff."

"Disruptions don't bother Jesus," Ponder says. "Remember

when he was trying to preach and that guy kept hollering out, 'Have mercy!'"

"Oh, yeah."

"How about when Mary Magdalene barged in on the board meeting or those boys cut a hole in the roof during church so they could lower their sick buddy down? Jesus get upset about that?"

"Guess you're right," I reply. "Didn't think about it that way."

"Jamie," he says, with a determined look, "Jesus doesn't care about a bunch of rules or appearances. He cares about people. I can come out to this dining hall and preach love and grace week after week. But I can't take it past these doors. Jesus needs people who can take it past the doors. Understand?"

I nod to Ponder and watch as he walks the long hall out. The charge nurse calls for evening meds as I stand there with my hand on the key.

Big Mike comes up from the side. "We can still play volleyball tonight?" he asks.

"I don't see why not. Help me get everybody together?"

"Sure," Big Mike says. "Hey, Jamie?"

"Yeah?"

"Thanks for taking us to church, man."

SEVEN

RAMBLE ON, OL' BLUE

*"Thank you for hiding [the truth] from
those who think themselves wise and clever,
and for revealing [it] to the childlike."*

—MATTHEW 11:25 NLT

THERE'S AN ALCOHOLIC IN THE INTAKE OFFICE WITH slicked-back white hair wearing a field jacket, filthy sneakers, and a T-shirt that says "Ask Me About My Grandkids."

"How 'bout them grandkids?" I ask.

He tents out the shirt and tilts his head down to read the print. "Ain't got none," he tells me. "Just a shirt somebody gimme."

He had had a good spell of sobriety but then his mother died from cancer of the brain. Then the sweet potato plant where he'd worked twenty-five years shut down and stole his pension. Then his wife left him for a gambling diesel mechanic. He didn't tell me any of this. His neighbor told me as he dropped off the guy's suitcase at the office door.

"He's a good-hearted old fella," the neighbor said before he left. "Hope y'all are able to get him in."

"His benefits are good, he smells like a whiskey barrel, and he wants to go," I tell the neighbor. "That's really all the criteria we need."

We're standing at the curb waiting for the hospital van. The alcoholic rocks back and forth, kicks against the asphalt a time or two, and finally says, "You ever just look around at life and wonder what in the world is goin' on down here?"

"Sure. Who don't?"

"Exactly. Even in the Bible, son. Every one of them characters in that book wondered the same thing at one point or another. If you ain't ever really read it close, check it out sometime. See for yourself."

When you're waiting for a ride to rehab at ten o'clock on a Sunday night, small talk can turn spiritual pretty quick.

"All right," I tell him. "I'll check it out."

"Like, whose idea was all this?" He holds out his hands like Moses before the sea and pivots from the Jiffy Lube to Taco Bell. "I ain't asked to be born. Ain't asked to die. Sure ain't asked to be judged. I ain't signed up for none of this. But here I am."

I like this guy. The long white hair and whiskers. He reminds me of Blue from the movie *Old School*. Might still be a little drunk, though.

"I hear you," I reply. Waiting on the van sucks. I didn't really want to get a call tonight. But ramble on, Ol' Blue. Just listening can be pretty peaceful when I let it roll.

He pulls a nickel from his pocket, staring at it and shining the silver with his thumbs.

"Even Jesus Christ hissself," he says, "wasn't so sure sometimes, was he?" Blue smiles easy, his face brighter, like the sun breaking free from dark clouds. "But I figure that's where that whole amazin' grace thing comes in. You know that song, don't ya?"

Blue stands on the sign post base and sings that part from the chorus starting with "*That saved a wretch like me . . .*"

"I know it," I say, waving him down. "How much you said you had to drink today?"

"I told you. Just one," he says, moving his hands from six inches to about two feet apart.

Blue sits back down beside me. A friend from college pulls up, waiting to turn right on red. She sees us, toots the horn, and waves. We wave back. Blue lays his head on my shoulder and lolls out his tongue. My classmate laughs, shakes her head, and pulls away.

"So anyway, my point is, you see," he says, sitting up straight, "maybe God said, 'Well, before I judge 'em too hard, I might oughta walk a mile in their shoes.'"

In Blue's world God talks a lot like the narrator on *The Dukes of Hazzard.*

"So he come down to earth as a little baby," Blue continues, "fought with brothers and sisters and worked in the family woodshop. Tried to go tell people the good news and his friends screwed him over and then—them religious folks kilt him."

"Never thought about it that way," I say.

"And maybe," says Blue, serious as he can muster, "when Jesus got back to heaven he kicked off them shoes, looked at God, and said, 'Dad, it's rough down there. Go easy on 'em.'"

I stare at him, wondering if the Lord has tricked me again. If he is showing me that truth comes from strange places—that for those willing to watch and listen, revelation is all around and everyplace is holy ground. Then again, Blue is sort of drunk and I am overly dramatic and rattled in the brain.

"How'd you come up with that?" I ask.

"I got lots of time to think," Blue says. "When you said that van was coming?"

"Any minute now."

"We best hurry then," he says, pointing to the liquor store down the street. "Get that half-pint you promised me for the trip."

"I don't remember promising you no half-pint."

"Oh, you did," he snorts. "Said your boss man would pay you back."

We make our way across the street and down, Blue walking sideways and talking with his hands, singing "Amazing Grace" and preaching about Jesus' shoes, trying to persuade me that what he really needs for the trip is an entire fifth.

But the sign at Lucky's Liquor Shack is dark.

"Sunday night," Blue explains.

"Aw, man. I'm sorry."

"You really thought the liquor store was gonna be open on Sunday?" He laughs. "You don't drink much, do ya?"

"Not really."

"That's okay," he teases, elbowing me in the side. "I'll be fine."

"You sure?" I'm checking his vitals as the van arrives.

"I'm sure," Blue says as he climbs through the sliding side door. "Enjoyed talking with you tonight."

"Me too," I tell him, wedging his suitcase behind the seat. "Come see me when you get home. I'll take you to lunch. We'll make the boss man pay."

"You got it, friend," he says. "I'll see you then."

I stand in Lucky's parking lot, watching as the van drives

away. Just before they pull onto the on-ramp, Blue turns and lifts his hand.

Truth came from a lot of strange places in the Bible. Perverts and murderers, prisoners and women of ill repute. Cheats and thieves and misfit carpenters. I hope that means God will show up anywhere, anyhow, through anyone. I hope that means nothing is wasted and everything works together for the good. I hope what Ol' Blue told me is true, that Jesus walked a mile in my shoes, that grace really is amazing, and that's why everything will be all right. That would be good news.

I'm glad Jesus' time on earth wasn't all elaborate or fancy. He was content to be common, just some working-class guy from a Podunk town who ignored the religious leaders and hung out with losers and loose women and sinners like me. Sometimes, when I worry about things, I think about that and it helps.

The streets are empty and traffic lights flash slow. I sit back on the bus bench by Lucky's front door. There's a feeling in the city late on a Sunday night, like the show is over and the credits have rolled. Like God slips in from his study, in his house shoes and tattered robe, reading glasses sliding down the end of his nose. I know God doesn't need reading glasses. I think he just wears them to put me at ease, so he seems like a trusted old friend I can talk to about anything at all. Like God just might leave heaven to come down and sit with me awhile, watching and listening while the whole world sleeps.

Sunday night late in the city. Feels like I'm the only person awake and alive. God peers over the top of his glasses, giving me a wink and a smile. Amazing grace. Everything's gonna be all right.

EIGHT

THE GOLDEN TICKETS OF GOD

"They called me a lush, a friend of the riffraff.
Opinion polls don't count for much, do they?"

—JESUS, MATTHEW 11:19 MSG

I'M FILLING OUT THE PAPERWORK FOR GRADUATION WHEN my advisor passes the office.

"Blaine, son, graduating, huh?" Dr. Stephens is a chubby little prof with woodpecker hair, thick gold-rimmed glasses, and a voice somewhere between Mr. Haney and Yogi Bear.

"Guess so," I reply. "So, uh . . . what can one do with a degree in psychology?"

"All kinds of things," he exclaims in his Jellystone meets *Green Acres* tone. "You could sell loafers, deliver newspapers, man a kiosk in the mall . . ." He slaps my back and his fuzzy eyebrows dance. "Have you thought about a future in cable TV installation?"

"Thanks for telling us this as we walk out the door."

"Or you could psych tech at the mental hospital," he suggests.

"Been there," I tell him. "A good while now."

"The state starts out caseworkers at twelve twenty-five an hour."

"Twelve twenty-five? I make more than that at Skate City."

"Does Skate City offer retirement and benefits?"

"No, sir."

"Well," he says, resting his chin in the web of flesh between his first finger and thumb, "you could just keep going."

"Seriously."

"I am serious. GRE's in two weeks. Give it a shot. What have you got to lose?"

Two hundred bucks. That's what I've got to lose. That's the fee to take the Graduate Records Exam, your golden ticket into grad school. I don't have two hundred dollars to spare. Besides, like I'm really going to be some counselor or psychologist? Smoking a pipe with my sweater-vest on, sitting around listening to people's problems all day? No thanks. I'm just a goofball—the guy who told the high school guidance counselor his dream job would be playing Tigger at Disney. But the Magic Kingdom's a long way away, and it's not like I've got anything else going on. So I do what bewildered, not-yet-ready-for-the-real-world students do. I fill out an application for graduate school.

Okay, Jesus, I pray. *If you really want me to do this, I'm gonna need a couple hundred bucks.* Sometimes it's easier to put things off on God. *By Monday,* I add, remembering the deadline to pay. *Thanks and amen.*

It's Thursday afternoon now. Two hundred extra dollars might as well be the moon. How much can really happen in three days?

"FIFTY BUCKS APIECE PLUS TIPS, TWO ONE-HOUR SETS, acoustic," says Spike. "You in?"

Spike is bone thin and legally blind, and he owns the record store just up the street. Severely diabetic and unable to drive, he could draw disability. But instead he works sixty hours a week, parties like a frat boy, and is the most live-life-to-the-fullest guy I know. He's got a regular Thursday night gig at a little hot spot near campus, but says he needs a partner with new songs.

"Lemme think about it," I tell him. "But yeah man, I need the cash."

I've been pretty active with church lately and gave up working in bars. But technically Spike's gig is not a bar. To be considerate, I let Marky, the youth pastor, know my plans.

"It's really just a coffeehouse," I explain. "In fact, that's the name. The Coffee House."

"Original," he says. "By the college, huh. They sell liquor?"

"Yeah. And, uh, you know. Coffee."

He smiles, just a little. "Do they sell more liquor or coffee?"

"Liquor," I confess.

"If you want to bless people with your talents we sure could use you down at Grace Place, brother." Marky's a good guy, only giving me a hard time. "Sing a little. Feed the hungry."

I hide my face with my hands and try to think of a good reason not to sing at the soup kitchen.

"The whole hairnet thing," I say, gesturing around my mop of curls.

"I got ya," Marky says, goosing my ribs. "Go do your thing."

The Coffee House is a dark, narrow space with low tables and slouchy old couches around the edges, just down from fraternity row, right between Hairport Beauty Salon and E-Z

Money Loans. Our stage is against the left wall by the door, about seven feet high and no bigger than a kitchen table at the top. A steep set of stairs with wrought-iron rails stands front and center.

"Who built our stage, the Mayans?" I ask.

"*Yes!*" Spike says, thrusting up his index and pinky fingers. "The *Mayans!*" He grabs a beer from the bar. "So what's the set list?"

"Side one of *Shotgun Willie*," I tell him, glancing over the meager crowd. "Side two of *G N' R Lies.*"

"Cool," he says.

"I'm joking."

We hike our gear to the summit and play Otis Redding and the Stones. Lenny Kravitz into Haggard. Anything really. Customers watch with heads pitched back like they're at a planetarium show. Between songs they clap politely. Someone yells out "*Skynyrd!*"

"Every single night," says Spike, rolling his eyes.

"I can fix this," I tell him.

I play a six-minute version of "Simple Man" just to keep the peace, but sure enough not two songs later some other clown shouts "*Skynyrd!*" again. To that we offer a long medley of "Mr. Banker" and "Curtis Loew" into "Stairway to Freebird." Nobody yells "*Skynyrd!*" after that.

It's forty minutes into the second set, busier than usual, and people are actually making a little ruckus for us between songs. A raven-haired beauty with Spanish eyes hauls herself up on stage.

"Hey! Hey, you," she says, giving my elbow a tug. She's wearing a black skirt and a shiny Western blouse that strains to contain her. A sketchy-looking guy waits at the bottom, eyeing her as she says, "Play me that song about the pony."

I stare at her, then to her fellow. He grins and gives me two thumbs up. The girl leans back against the rail and stifles a belch. "Whoa," she says. "'Pony,' you gotta play it for me, okay?"

"I've got, like, an acoustic guitar here." I lift it to prove my point.

"'Pony' is my most *fav'rite* song. *Ever.*" She whispers this like it's a secret you'd climb a Chinese mountain to hear.

Two college girls at the table stage left start whooping. "Play it!" shouts a thin, tall blonde.

"Yeah!" the smaller blonde chimes in.

Sketchy Guy steps up, a five-dollar bill between his first two fingers. "Cowgirl here's a dancer," he explains. "Sang it for her, would ya?"

I look to Spike, deep into his third Zima Gold. He holds up the bottle and waggles his head, his binocular glasses refracting the red and purple spotlights.

"All right!" he says.

"Pony! Pony!" the coeds chant. Sketchy Guy winks and lays the cash on top of my guitar case. "Just play it, bro."

Good grief. What have I gotten myself into now?

"Key of A minor," I call, kicking off the beat as Spike joins in and Cowgirl begins to snap her fingers and swish her hair. I wave the college girls on stage to help me sing. They stumble up, smelling like two-for-one tap beer and Designer Imposters body spray.

"Who-ooo!" Tall Blonde croaks into the mic, knocking our guitars with her bony knees. Spike wobbles right and gestures for me to sing. I clear my throat, pull the mic in tight, and give it my best Conway Twitty growl.

If you're country
come prove it
help me catch my
Shetland pony

Small Blonde eyes me from the side and punches my arm, hard. "That ain't the words!"

"Quiet, blondie," I hiss. "Or make up your own."

Spike finds his groove between beatbox and acoustic guitar; Tall Blonde and Small sway side to side and sing some garble about sweaty saddles and sweet apples in the spring. A hush falls over the room as Cowgirl starts to dance.

We make our fifty and another forty apiece in tips. Spike disappears while I'm playing the night out, singing about that long train coming, urging the people to get ready, reminding us all that there's just no hiding against the Kingdom's Throne.

Sister Cowgirl's had too much Kahlúa, and Sketchy has to lead her away by the arm. At the door she breaks free, kisses her fingers, and holds them out to me. I catch her kisses and throw them out over the room as the last stragglers cheer. Sketchy gives me one last thumbs-up just before he tucks her into the waiting car.

In the parking lot after the show, Tall Blonde watches as Small Blonde steadies herself against my shoulder and tries to get her shoes back on. "I gotta quit all this drinkin'," Tall says in a scratchy voice.

"Shua, me," Small agrees, poking a finger into her own chest.

"Girl," Tall tells her friend, with the sort of truthful tone that comes to Southern girls when the liquor begins to wane. "We *need* to be gettin' our behinds back to church."

"I know that's right," Small replies.

"Hey," I say. "Come on, we'll all go."

Small Blonde flutters her lids and tries to focus around my face, her milk cow eyes slitted now.

"I likes your hair," she says, reaching out to pet me like a spaniel. She makes a sudden sour face, covering her mouth, then shakes it off and smiles. "What your name was again?"

———

I SHOW UP TO GRACE PLACE THE NEXT AFTERNOON, TUCK my hair under a hat, and throw half my tips into the offering box.

Seed money for the GRE, I tell Jesus. *You uh, might want to wash it first.*

"Brother J! Glad you could make it!" Marky strides over, his bright Christian smile shining like the morning sun. "You got friends coming, huh?"

I point to the big picture window just past the serving tables. A silver pickup pulls up and parks. Two blondes in sweatpants and ponytails make their way through the door. When they spot me, the lanky girl bats her lashes while the shorter one throws up her hands and sashays across the room to where we stand.

"Oh, Lordy," Marky says and everybody laughs.

"Pastor," I reply, "meet my friends."

NINE

GOLDEN TICKETS II, THE FIRST CLUE

"And suddenly there came a sound from heaven as of a rushing mighty wind."

−ACTS 2:2 KJV

I GOT AN EXTRA TWENTY IN CASH FRIDAY NIGHT BECAUSE the rink was so busy, but it's Sunday now and I'm still about a hundred dollars short. I've heard it said the Lord is sometimes late but always on time. Or something like that. Anyway, the phone rings.

"You goin' to church tonight?" Caleb asks. Caleb's straight country, a tiny guy with an apple-pie smile and heart the size of Texas. He grew up Charismatic but with enough confidence and humor to take it all in stride.

"Planned on it," I reply. "Why?"

"Living Water asked me to play their revival. Just a couple songs before the evangelist does his thing. You wanna come sing?"

"Living Water out by the chicken plant?" I ask. "They're, like, super Holy Roller, right?"

"That's the one," he says. "They blow the roof off."

"Sure," I tell him. "Why not?"

Caleb picks me up and we drive out to the church, carrying our guitars across a dark and empty sanctuary toward the front. There's a giant banner stretched over the altar, script in bold italics, the words like a warning or a call to watch.

THE SON OF MAN COMES LIKE A THIEF IN THE NIGHT!

We're off to the side tuning up when the reverend steps up to us, his countenance stern.

"Talk to you boys in my office a minute?"

The music minister trails behind him, his lightbulb head bald and shiny on top, the sides and back ringed with baby-fine hair. He narrows his lizard eyes and gives us a look of utter disgust.

The reverend shuts the door behind us and shakes his head, looking like Andy Rooney with Roosevelt's mustache. "We do not allow rock and roll in this church," he declares.

"Well, uh, no sir," Caleb explains. "We play a, um . . . a good old gospel sound. But you know . . ." He pats me on the back. "Really sold out for church."

"For church," I agree, my elbow slung around Caleb's skinny neck. There's a mirror on the back wall and I steal a glimpse. Caleb favors Opie and I look like a roadie for Guns N' Roses.

The music minister stands with hands on his hips, beaming like a snitch. The reverend leans in, speaking to Caleb but glaring at me. "There will be *no rock and roll* in this house. You all understand, now?"

Caleb nods.

"Yes, sir," I agree.

Scolded, we drag our tails back to the sanctuary. The church is jam-packed with old-school Holy Rollers, men with crew cuts in long-sleeved white shirts and high-water slacks, women with no makeup or jewelry, hair pinned and piled high, dresses to the floor.

"Welcome to 1955," Caleb says.

An angry deacon announces us and we take the stage, backed by the house praise band. I step to the mic. Feedback shrills. A legion of eyeballs give me the stink.

Caleb leans in and whispers, "Do your thing, Jamie. You sing first."

I count it down and we kick hard into "I Saw the Light," double time from Hank, heavy on the backbeat, with driving guitars. Thirty seconds pass. A minute. The reverend stands and starts to jig. People spill out into the aisles, clapping on the two and four. Shouts go up, a woman with a big gray bun begins to keen; the church breaks loose, speaking in tongues, pogo-ing, gripping the pew backs, praising the Lord and wailing red-faced at Satan to *"Get thee behind!"*

As Caleb takes the verse, a small, dark-skinned man steps into the space between the pews. He raises both hands, jerks, and glossolalia gushes forth. Another man moves in, just behind him to the right. He slips off his shoes, lies facedown on the floor, and starts to weep.

We pick up the pace and medley into "Jesus on the Mainline." I sing it with full-on fever, sweating through my coat jacket, hair in my eyes. A woman in a bluejean skirt and white Keds runs full speed from front to back with one finger lifted high.

"*Hoah!*" she shouts at the corners. "*Glo-ray!*"

A seventy-something-year-old man with a greasy black comb-over dances around the side rows and up past the platform. As he passes, he pulls out a harmonica and blows furious notes, every one in time and tune. Caleb shoots up his eyebrows, grins wide, and we lean back-to-back while he slings a flurry of notes from his guitar.

I search the crowd for the music minister. He stands to the side, swaying, hands held high, eyes tightly shut, his bald dome shining in the light.

We shamble and crash to an end. The evangelist storms the pulpit and motions for us to jump back in. We find the groove again as the little firecracker of a man with flame-red hair and a forest-green suit paces the platform and heads down into the aisles, shouting his riff like Coltrane against the beat.

"*Jesus* is here."

"Jesus *is* here."

"Jesus is *here!*"

Then like a cross between Jimmy Swaggart and Muhammad Ali:

"*Get up on your feet and make welcome the Alpha and Omega, the First and Last, Rose of Sharon, Lily of the Valley, Lion of Judah, Lamb of God, Prince of Peace, King of Kings and Lord of Lords, the Bread of Life and Bright Mornin' Star . . .*"

The evangelist pauses; a sound like tornadoes fills the room.

"*JESUS! IS! HERE!*"

The congregation goes apocalyptic; we wait for the roof to blow, for bloodred moons and crashing stars, for lightning to split the eastern sky and rapture us over the jasper wall.

After the service, Caleb and I sit behind the baptismal pool, quiet and dazed, still amazed at everything we just experienced. The reverend slips into the tiny space, lays his palm on Caleb's shoulder, and presses his hand into mine.

"Hal-le-lu-jah," he says. "The Lord bless and keep you both."

He leaves the room. I open my hand. There is a thick wad of bills.

Caleb laughs and sweeps the air with the flat of his hand.

"There'll be *no rock and roll* in this house."

MONDAY MORNING I PAY MY FEES AT THE REGISTRAR, AND somehow between grace and blind faith, I crush the GRE and score in the top five percentile. But the lady in the financial aid office informs me there'll be no money for graduate school.

"You already borrowed a ton in undergrad," she says. "And honey, once you get that first diploma, they're done."

I'm walking back across campus, running through my options. Maybe being the cable guy wouldn't be so bad. That van seems kinda cool. I cannot sell shoes. I bet if I practiced a little I could ride a motorcycle in one those big steel ball cages at the circus.

Okay, God, I pray. *Now what?* Halfway through the quad, I run into the head of education, Dean Gage.

"Hear you're thinking about a master's," he says. Gage's daughter is a teenage rink rat. Good kid—kinda shy. I helped her learn to skate backward.

"Nah, they just told me," I reply, jerking my thumb toward financial aid. "No more cash."

"So what are you going to do now?"

"Sir," I tell him. "I do not have the first clue."

"Tell you what. Meet me in my office in thirty minutes, and let's see what we can do."

One hour later, I walk out into the sun with a fully paid graduate assistantship and a tag to park ten steps from the psychology department's front door. Not only are my tuition and books covered, they're going to pay me to go to school.

Wolcott Hall stands on the water's edge. I walk around back and watch the paddleboats stream by, trying to sort it out in my mind.

An hour ago the only plan I could come up with was try to go full-time at Forest Hills Psych. That or find a regular shift back in rock radio. I figured I'd have to quit the rink. Settle in. Grow up.

Can I even make it in grad school? Even if I do pass and graduate with a master's in psychology, could I ever be a serious psychologist? The kind that gives people advice on how to live their lives? Me?

You know that part in the Bible where Jesus says, "Give no thought to tomorrow"? That's one command I've followed pretty well thus far.

Well, God, I pray, skipping flat stones across the water. *Here we go.*

PART TWO

STRANGERS AND ANGELS UNAWARE

*"I turned to examine wisdom,
insanity, and foolishness."*

–ECCLESIASTES 2:12 ISV

*"A watchman is an important person,
but he doesn't do very much."*

–EUGENE PETERSON

TEN

INTO THE VENT

*"Laughter is the closest thing
to the grace of God."*

–KARL BARTH

NOW THAT I'M IN GRAD SCHOOL, FOREST HILLS PSYCH steps me up to more crisis intake work and less time on the ward. Florentine calls me in to cover the outreach office for the afternoon while he's out of town. I rummage through my hamper and put together the kind of outfit a homeless man might wear if asked to meet the mayor. Wrinkled khakis I picked up for $2.99 at the Goodwill off St. John, a button-down shirt with ink stains on the cuff, a size or two too big.

For an hour I sit, spinning in the office chair and staring at Florentine's calendar from *Hot Rod* magazine. For the second hour I lie on the floor. Just as I'm drifting off, the door flies open and the building manager storms in.

"Where's Florentine?" he asks.

"West Texas," I tell him, sitting up.

"Who are you?"

"Night guy."

"There's a girl in trouble in the office next door. Can you go?"

"Where?"

"Next door."

"At the bank building?"

"Yes," he says, impatient now. "Hurry. *Go*."

I make my way to the third floor of the bank, through reception, and past some cubicles to the back. Two ladies are waiting, a black woman in a pantsuit and a younger girl in a short, red skirt and white heels.

"What happened?" I ask.

"Jada. She got some call and started freaking out and climbed in the wall."

I hunch down and peer into the hole.

"What is this," I ask, "some kind of vent or something?"

"Yeah, she's back there," says Pantsuit. "Her and her man been having some problems."

"Jada, the guy's here, honey," White Heels calls through the hole.

"I ain't climbin' in there," I tell them. Both women shoot me a harsh look. "Y'all call the cops?" I ask.

"Look, she don't need to be arrested, she needs help," says Pantsuit.

White Heels adds, "You're a counselor, right? She needs somebody to talk to."

"I'm not a counselor," I tell her. "I'm just the crisis guy."

"Hello?" White Heels says, gesturing to the wall. "I think we got a crisis here."

I lean down and gaze back into the vent, then stand up again. "I'm not climbing in that hole."

A bulbous man with strands of white running through the sides of his hair steps up to us. "Listen," he says, with a supervisor's tone. "I'm going to have to call an ambulance."

"Kent," Pantsuit grunts, "not yet. This here man's from crisis."

There's a cell phone clipped to the belt of Kent's navy Sansabelt slacks. He gives me a quick once-over and presses his palm to his forehead.

"I'm claustrophobic," I explain.

"Forget this," says White Heels, twisting off her shoes and tossing them to the side. "Jada, baby," she calls down the hole, "I'm a come in there. You hold on."

She gives me an ugly glare and tugs at her skirt. "All the days to wear a dress," she grumbles, scrunching down with one hand holding the hem of her garment.

"Wait, wait," I tell her. "You sure she doesn't have any weapons?"

"What's she gonna have? A stapler?"

"I mean no razor blades or knives or anything?"

A voice comes from back in the hole. "I don't have nothin'."

I look into their faces one by one. Then I kneel down and crawl into the hole. Made-for-TV movie: Misfit Psych Guy saves jilted woman from the . . . collapsed mine shaft. Who will they cast for my role? Probably that guy who played Napoleon Dynamite.

I scooch through on my elbows. It's not so bad, actually. It's not really a vent, but some sort of low-paneled crawl space. The gap gets bigger at the end. A girl sits with her back against the wall. She's sort of pug dog cute and reminds me of the TV chef Rachel Ray. If Rachel Ray let herself go a little. It's kinda dim back here.

"Thanks for coming," she says, sarcastic-like. She's crying, blotting her face with a wadded-up tissue.

"I'm claustrophobic," I explain.

"I heard you out there," she says. "You didn't have to crawl up in here. I'm fine."

"Your friends don't think so."

"Yeah, well."

"What happened?"

She starts to explain and breaks down crying into the Kleenex. After a while she squeaks out the words: "Tucker, he called and said he's leavin'. Took all his stuff, said he's leavin' me for Tammie."

"Who's Tammie?"

Jada blows her nose and takes a long breath in.

"Some skeeze at the tanning salon," she says.

"Sorry to hear that."

"Calls me at work like he knows I ain't gonna freak out here, like what am I gonna do, right?"

"So you crawled back here."

"I was crying so hard. When I was a little girl we used to have a space like this through my bedroom closet. I used to sit there when the storms come. It calmed me."

"You didn't see this coming?"

"I been through a lot this year. Doctor got me on antide-pressants, sleeping pills. Still don't sleep half the time." Then, in a quieter voice, "Sometimes I tell the girls I'm goin' to lunch and come sit back here and pray and stuff, try to get my mind to calm down. I'll be fine. I just don't want to go out there right now. Everybody needs to just let me chill."

"You don't want to hurt yourself, do you?"

Voices buzz from down the hole. Something about an ambulance on the way. One of the women says Jada's mother is on the line.

Jada rests her head against the wall. "I don't think so," she says. "What is this place?"

"Used to stack files back here," she says. "Not us. People here before us."

I sit back against the opposite wall and stretch out my legs.

"One time I had a crush on this girl. Bekka Rooney," I say. "Invited her to my birthday party; all my friends are there. I'm totally smitten. Right in front of everybody she says I'm a skinny monkey with a big ugly nose. I climbed the big elm in the back-yard and hid the rest of the day. Birthday cake and candle time came, but they couldn't find me. I didn't want to be around nobody. Needed some time."

"So she called you a monkey and you climbed a tree?"

"Pretty much."

Jada nods her head. "You remember what it feels like then."

"Sure," I tell her. "That party was just last year."

She spits out laughter and presses the Kleenex to her eyes. "What, you get paid to crawl in holes and make crazy people laugh?"

"Ah, you're not crazy," I tell her. "Just having a hard time."

"Jada," Pantsuit's voice calls. "Ambulance is here, baby."

Jada hangs her head and squeaks out a single, tiny curse.

"All right, look," I tell her. "We can't sit in this hole all day. You're gonna have to go with the ambulance guys. Or go with me."

"Yeah, yeah, I know. I need to get some help," she says. "So if I go, will you be my counselor?"

"I'm not a counselor."

"What are you?"

I don't answer. From outside the hole, radios squawk, more voices add to the mix. Jada laughs again and shakes her head.

"Okay," she says. "Let's go."

ELEVEN

LIFE IS CRAZY / AMAZING GRACE

*"Truthfulness itself is almost medicinal, even
when it's served without advice or insight."*

–AUGUSTEN BURROUGHS

SATURDAY NIGHT CHURCH. I'M SITTING IN THE BALCONY, grateful to be escaping the harsh gloom of Sunday morning. I don't mean to sound sacrilegious, but I have never, ever liked Sundays.

The praise band is playing a slow-building song about power and majesty and mountains bowing down. There's a lady in the space between the pulpit and the pews with her shoes off, swaying and walking in circles. She's wearing a grey dress flecked with little yellow flowers—not vintage, just old. The band crescendos into the chorus, and the woman falls to her knees with tears streaming. Her stockings are torn and the soles of her feet are dirty. She lifts her hands and they tremble.

Sometimes I wonder if I attend a Charismatic church just

for the emotional fireworks show, only because I'm interested in the intersection of faith and humanity, religious spectacle and struggle on display. It's a strange mix, studying behavioral psychology and going to a Holy Roller church.

College professors caution me about preachers, saying they are frequently power hungry and repressed, prone to manipulation, peddling shallow spirituality to cookie-cutter robots too scared and apathetic to think for themselves. Preachers warn me about college professors, stating they are often grandiose blowhards, infecting young, supple minds with their arrogant skepticisms. Best I can tell, there's truth to both assumptions. But I'm hoping for a balanced way, that each can bring the other up, and all things can work together for the good.

As the praise band fades and plays low, the platform goes dark and the words *Cardboard Testimonies* glow from the big center screen. A short video explains that church members will walk onto the stage and hold up cardboard signs with a few words written about who they were before, then turn the sign over to show how their lives have been changed.

The screen goes black and a spotlight hits the stage. A middle-aged woman walks up wearing too much makeup and an unshapely blouse. She holds a sign that states:

TRAPPED BY ANXIETY AND FEARS.

Just before she flips the sign, her eyes move down and away. The other side says:

SET FREE. ALIVE NOW IN HIS PRESENCE.

There's an awkward pause as she stands waiting. A staff member with a headset directs the woman toward the back of the stage. She lowers her sign to the side and the staff member cues her to raise it again. The praise band laps through the chorus, slow and emotional, as people stream through with their signs.

BROKEN. ABUSED. HOPELESS.
TRUSTING. BELIEVING. DELIVERED.

I scan the signs quickly but mostly watch for what the eyes show, if the stories on their faces line up with the words on the signs. Observation is the key to good psychology. Everything tells a story. But truth often hides. You have to watch without bias, devoted to the pursuit of information and not just confirmation for what you already wish to believe. That's what they teach us in school.

Any honest preacher or half-baked psychologist would tell you there's a balance between healthy skepticism and being a crank. Change is more action than emotion. For instance, if you quit drinking or taking drugs and maintained sobriety for a reasonable length of time, that could be marked as change. But feeling changed isn't change.

Many of the testimonies on the signs are too subjective, the language too vague. There's nothing to measure but intent.

There's a healing televangelist I watch sometimes. In every program someone comes to the stage and the announcer states something like, "This woman has been addicted to crack cocaine for five years but says tonight she felt something break loose inside! She says she feels totally delivered from the chains of cocaine!"

The woman will stand there crying, and I'm sure at some level what she feels is real. But feeling delivered and living sober are two different things. I've spent too many nights at the rehab and psych ward to think about it any other way. I've seen too many people wanting results without the struggle and the work. In most cases, God changes us through the struggle and the work.

It's probably cynical of me to be sitting up here analyzing all these signs. But I once heard a prophet say, "If you'll scratch a cynic, you'll find a disappointed idealist." I want badly for it all to be true, to see miracle changes and happy endings and for God to fix us—in this life, now. Perhaps I should not be studying behavioral psych.

But I am. And truth is still truth, even if you find it covered in dirt and rust. All truth is God's truth. And there's hope in that too.

A weary-looking man in a blue dress shirt and loosely knotted tie walks slowly across the stage and holds up his sign.

PRAYED TEN YEARS FOR A CHILD.

THREE MISCARRIAGES.

BROKEN HEARTS.

He lets the sign linger before turning it around. There are no words on the other side. Only an arrow pointing stage left. The sweetest smile breaks across his face as a woman steps from the wings with a curly-headed baby on her hip. And when the baby laughs, the congregation stands, cheering and lifting their hands. So I stand and clap too. To honor truth and beauty. To let God know I still believe.

At last Pastor Reddy takes the stage and talks to us about

how a walk with Jesus will revolutionize your life and calm your raging seas.

"What would your sign say?" Reddy asks, holding up a piece of cardboard with a question mark on the front and back. "What will your story be?"

My sign would have to talk about struggle and doubt and hoping for the good. About making seventeen trips around the same mountain knowing you probably won't ever get it all figured out. About some change for the better and some for the worse, and sometimes not being able to tell the difference until you've traveled a long way down the road. Learning the hard way to watch and be still. Wrestling with a God I cannot understand.

Guess I would need a really big sign. But the truth is, every person in this room needs a giant sign. We need banners and boxes and pockets stuffed with tiny scraps of paper to tell the story of our train-wreck lives. One long procession of people trying to change, busted and broken but still fighting to keep hope alive.

Part of me wants to tell the pastor we need more balance in these displays. That it's wrong to reduce struggle and change and something as wild as a walk with God to a few words on a sign, to try and fit your messy story inside that small neat cardboard square as if Jesus always magically fixes everything and colors inside the lines. False hope can be more destructive than honest doubt. For the people here who have prayed a thousand prayers and still battle with addiction or depression or divorce, for that couple in the third row who have hoped and prayed for a very long time now and still don't have a child. Because I'm watching their faces too.

I would tell the preacher that what we should really do is just let people be real. But those cardboard testimonies might read more like:

BROKEN / BUT HOPEFUL
CRUSHED / BUT STILL HERE
STRUGGLING / AND STRUGGLING STILL
LIFE IS CRAZY / AMAZING GRACE

And what would really be wonderful and graceful is if the congregation would applaud those signs too. We could meet each other in the space between the altar and the pews and, for just a few sweet moments, be who we really are.

"Bow your heads with me please," Reddy says. "And let's pray."

I pray but with head up and eyes open, looking out over the crowd. The lady with the anxiety and fears sign keeps her head up too. Our eyes meet across the room. She tucks her sign away and slips quickly off stage. I cut through the back exit and pass her in the hall.

"Hey there," I say. "You all right?"

"I'm okay," she says. "Just don't like crowds."

"Me neither," I tell her. "Took a lot of courage to go up there. If I did it, I'd need a lot bigger sign."

"Yeah, I hear you," she replies. "But that's the size they gave me."

"I bet there's a lot more to your story than what's on the sign."

"Whole lot," she says, forcing a smile.

There's a gawky silence, impatient as the praise band sings and people stream to the altars. "I need to run," she says, and we exit through different doors.

I drive down a side road and cut across Seventh Street toward the river. At the red light I spot a figure slinking through the parking lot of Lucky's Liquor Store. It's her. Hard to keep secrets in a small town. Not really the sort of serendipitous moment I was looking for tonight.

Dear God in heaven, I pray. *Help us all.*

As I drive on it eats at me that I should turn back. And do what? *I am not the world's psych tech,* I tell the Lord.

Really now? he replies. *Says who?*

One thing about arguing with Jesus: you're not gonna change his mind. So after five or ten rounds of going back and forth with God, I finally whip the truck around, drive back, and park next to Lucky's neon sign.

Now what?

Don't embarrass her, Jesus says.

"Just how am I s'posed to do that?" I ask, out loud now, and a little irate. "And why do you only talk to me when it's some crazy, inconvenient, awkward thing you need me to do? How about some Powerball numbers? Or sending some hot young well-adjusted church chick my way? Would that be too hard, huh? Is my whole life gonna be one sad parade of psych ward cigarettes, liquor stores, and bad tattoos? Hello? Jesus?"

My side window is a quarter way down. This dude comes strolling through the lot wearing a satin jacket, sunglasses, and disco pants, looking like some long-lost, black-sheep Doobie Brother, like that black-sheep Doobie Brother who still lives at home with Doobie Mama. He stoops low to look when he hears my rant.

"Don't drink and drive, brother," he warns cheerfully, pointing double fingers to me before he ducks through Lucky's door.

Great. At the Holy Roller church I'm Dr. Psychology and now at the liquor store I'm rolling so holy I sound drunk.

Real funny, Jesus, I pray. *Ha, ha.*

Searching Lucky's picture window, I find my church lady perusing giant jugs of Gallo wine at the endcap on aisle four. I wait until she pays and leaves the register, step out of my truck and start walking toward the door.

"Hey there. Wow," I say when we meet. "You shop here too?"

"Just a little something for my stomach," she says in a sheepish voice. "This is the last, I swear."

"I hear ya," I reply. "Sometimes it's like, Jesus, can you help me turn the wine back into water?" It's the only lighthearted thing I can think of to say. Heard it in a country song. She laughs, thank God. So I laugh too.

"Listen," I tell her, in a more serious tone. "I work at a place that helps people with like, you know, anxiety and drinking and stuff. If there's anything I can do."

She studies me awhile before replying. "You got a number where I can call you?" she asks. "I wouldn't want nobody at the church to know."

"Sure thing," I say, scribbling my number on the side of her bag. "Just let me know. We all need a little help now and then."

"I will," she says, shaking my hand. "You be careful now."

I head into the store and loiter around the lottery ticket rack awhile. There's a row of those Spanish candles behind the counter with Jesus on the side, so I stare at him and nod toward the Powerball display. No such luck. Jesus is aloof now, busy ascending so it seems. *Never mind.*

Brother Doobie sidles up with a four-pack of coolers, plucks a burnt weenie from the Hot Dog Ferris Wheel, and slides it into a bun. Big letters on the back of his satin jacket read, "KKAS, HOME OF THE ROCK."

"Hey," I tell him. "I used to DJ there."

"No way!" he says, slurping spilled mustard from the side of his hand. "What was your name, man?"

"DJ Jamie James."

Doobie snaps his fingers and gives me the double point again. "Late-night guy," he cries, arms around me right there in the liquor store. "Man, I used to listen to you all the time. You got me through a lot of long nights . . ."

Life is so crazy. Stages and phases, stories and struggle and change. Jesus walking on water and through the walls, ascending and coming down. Sometimes it feels like God left us stranded, and other times it's like he's everywhere you look. Seems the best we can do is take it as it comes, living one small moment at a time.

"Late-night guy," I reply, hugging Brother Doobie back. "Yeah, my man, that's me."

TWELVE

BROTHER JOHN AND THE RAGGED STRAGGLERS BAND

*"I want to go back to believing everything
and knowing nothing at all."*

—FRANK WARREN

A SPEAKER AT SUNDAY SERVICE NEARLY MAKES THE whole church cry.

"There's a man here tonight. Sir, I don't know your name but you've been battling a long time. In fact, you came here tonight to give God one last chance to come through. You've got the pistol to end your life in the glove compartment of your car."

Brother John steps from the pulpit to the floor.

"I've been there, friend. I drank that whiskey. I smoked that cocaine. I held that pistol." He takes out his handkerchief, wipes away the sweat, and sadly shakes his head.

"Sir, I don't know your name—but I know *Someone* who knows your name. And he is saying *it's not over*. You can make your way to this altar and get your heart and life right with God, tonight."

The air is electric and the weight heavy in our chests. Brother John's voice breaks. "*Come home.*" In the second row, a woman cries out.

A man with big bifocals and a checkered shirt stands and walks the aisle, his face drawn and legs heavy, as if he is wading through deep water a long way toward the shore.

"All across this room there are people who have been putting on a front and living a lie, like everything is all right," Brother John says. "But inside you fight a losing battle. A war against depression, against thoughts of suicide. Some of you take too many pills, some of you drink yourself to sleep and you think nobody knows, *nobody knows . . .*"

He pauses, his sad eyes scanning the room. "Come home."

"*Come home, come home,*" the choir sings. Slowly, people stream toward the altars.

"Come home, sir. Come home, ma'am. Come home, teenager— there is no judgment for you here; only mercy and grace. Come home." Brother John walks through those gathered at the front, touching heads and shoulders as he passes by.

I lean against the balcony rail, watching close. After the service I shake Brother John's hand. It is warm and soft, like well oiled leather.

"That was awesome, Brother John," I tell him.

"God is awesome," he says. "John Rayburn is just a man."

Three weeks later, at nearly one in the morning, I get a call from the sheriff to the psych ward's front door. They bring in a man, disheveled and barefoot, smelling like hard liquor. He glances at me for a moment, then back to the floor.

"John," I say.

He nods. "I know you?"

I lead him back, saying nothing more. I give Brother John food and fresh clothes and take him out to smoke. Never once do I mention church.

He stubs out his second cigarette and stares at me for a long time. A dim light shines in his eyes, like a lone porch light at the far end of a gravel lane.

"I know you," he says.

WHAT DO YOU DO WHEN THE PREACHER SHOWS UP drunk and desperate at the psych ward door? I do not know. Really, I don't. Sometimes it seems there's no clear meaning to these things, and the ending you get doesn't make sense. When that happens, all I know to do is stick to the small, simple things. To bring Brother John food and clothes and make sure he knows he's in a safe place to be honest, to deal with his story, and to work through whatever hard truths he needs to face. If you look at it that way, some lock-down, dead-end psych ward could be like a church too. If you want to rise above, we're here to help. But we refuse to pretend. We will not deny the hard truths.

Come to think of it, Jesus could have picked the best and brightest to be in his original disciple band. Jesus isn't bound to time and circumstance, so I suppose he could have chosen Einstein, Steve Jobs, Abe Lincoln, and Billy Graham. He could have selected Shakespeare, Faulkner, Hemingway, and Stephen King to write the four gospels. Walt Disney. That would have been a good guy to have in the band. Or valedictorians from

Wheaton and Harvard Divinity School. A sharp, young group of twelve go-getters.

But God didn't do that. He picked roughneck fishermen and tax cheats. Liars and thieves. Outlaws and wild women. Jesus was willing to work with the people no one else wanted on their team. He chose flawed, messed-up, messy people. Just like Brother John. Just like me.

I suppose that means Jesus isn't that concerned with résumés. You don't need a seminary degree or dazzling charm or twin rows of perfect, white teeth. You don't have to be some hotshot preacher, motivational speaker, superstar athlete, born-again celebrity, or pumped-up type A extrovert. The only thing Jesus ever asked was, "Will you follow me?"

And he told the church crowd straight-up: "I didn't come for the religious people; I came for the misfits." Jesus doesn't show up looking for the supersaints and the spotless apostles of god-less optimism. He comes for the stragglers and the ragged and the screw-ups and the down-and-out.

Church doesn't make you feel welcome? "Come on," says Jesus, "I've got a place for you." Still struggling and confused and given to fits of lust or despair or anger and doubt? "Come on." Still rough around the edges? "Come on." Jesus still runs with a rough crowd.

It's a hard fall for Brother John, but sometimes good can come from bad situations. If nothing else, humility. Didn't Noah come straight from a mission trip and knock back a bottle of wine one time? Or something like that?

I don't know why things are so strange and difficult, why we are all so weird and broken behind closed doors. I don't know why God doesn't make life easier, why prayers don't work like magic, why it seems we spend our whole lives wandering in circles and fumbling with locked doors, trying to figure out some halfway decent way to live before it's time to die. I do not know. Maybe that's what faith is—living with the ends frayed and loose, hoping for things unseen, searching for something beyond what we can understand.

Truth is, we are all misfits and ragged stragglers. None of us are above the worst. But if you look at it right, that's good news. We all need rescue. We're all in the same boat. We help each other down here.

THIRTEEN

IN YOUR DREAMS

"Dare to be naïve."

–BUCKY FULLER

NIKKI THE FLOOR GUARD MEETS ME AT THE ROLLER RINK
door and holds up her hands.

"Major crisis," she declares.

"What?" I ask, gearing into adrenaline mode. "What is it?"

"Brittany's birthday cake didn't get delivered."

I laugh like a jackal, drive to the grocery store with my skates
still on, and roll through the bakery until I find a ready-made red
velvet cake with puppies and rainbow butterflies.

"Give me five minutes, baby," the cake lady says, "and I'll pipe
the kid's name on top. No extra charge."

The cake lady's a plump little woman, fat cheeks and flour in
her hair. She looks exactly like the lady who makes cakes at a small-
town Piggly Wiggly should. Like someone's sweet favorite aunt.

"Cool. I can wait," I reply. "The Pig treating you pretty good these days?"

"Honey, I taught third grade for thirty years," she says. "That was good and fine but I always did love to bake. It's a simple little dream but I'm happy."

"Happy is good."

"Happy is *real* good," Aunt Piggly says with a big, beaming, sweet aunt smile. "So what do you need this cake to say?"

"Happy Birthday Brittany."

"One *T* or two?"

"Two," I tell her.

"Five minutes," she says, turning, then back. "Do you like peanut butter? And cheesecake?"

"Who don't like peanut butter and cheesecake?"

She reaches into the oven, pulls out a cookie, and hands it to me. "Just made 'em hot," she says. "While you're waitin'." And with that, Aunt Piggly grabs her pastry bag and off she goes to pipe.

There are moments in life to stop and plant a flag. Take a picture in your mind so you won't soon forget. I'm on roller skates at the Piggly Wiggly bakery with a peanut butter cheesecake cookie in hand. Shoppers are scattered here and there but the store is mostly vacant. I've got five minutes to kill. So I take my cookie and roll through produce, back along frozen, and up aisle five.

The assistant manager stops me on six, right by the dryer sheets.

"Out*stand*ing idea," he says, sincerely enthused. "The work I could get done if I wore skates. Think you can teach me?"

I carry a pocketful of free passes so I slide one into his hand.

"One way to find out," I tell him. "Come on over."

I like just being the skating-rink guy sometimes. There is no such thing as depression or addiction at Skate City. You know what a suicide is at the roller rink? Coke, Sprite, Dr. Pepper, and Fanta Orange, mixed in the same cup.

Addiction? To what, Laffy Taffy?

I have never once dreaded going to work at the rink. Never remember having a bad day. Never stayed home sick. It's the lights and music, the wind in your hair and wheels beneath your feet, the smell of hot popcorn and sound of little kids laughing. Little kids laughing is the voice of God.

The Piggly Wiggly in-store radio is playing "Cool Change," and I'm rolling backward down aisle thirteen. There's a bleary-eyed old bag boy with straggly silver hair and a Wolfman beard, mopping a spot where someone dropped a pickle jar.

"All right, skate dude," he howls, high-fiving as I pass. "Watch the pickle juice."

Sometimes I think I could spend the rest of my life just being the roller-rink guy. Open my own place in some exotic locale like Cancun or Gulf Shores, Alabama. A roller rink across the street from the ocean. You ever do that thing where you dream about what the perfect life looks like? Dolphin Beach Roller Rink. Little cottage right next door. Waking up late morning, waves crashing against the shore. Walking to work. What is work? Disco balls and birthday parties. Rolling through the grocery store to pick up Brittany's cake. Spinning cotton candy and teaching kids to skate. Closing down at nine. Walking the beach late at night. I like that midnight Jesus, when you can talk to him just like a friend.

"Is there a place for Jesus in your dreams?" I heard an evangelist ask that once. In your secret dreams, does Jesus have a place? The Jesus I believe in does. He's like an old friend, closer than a brother, that person you can tell anything to. Jesus won't laugh at your dreams or roll his eyes or make you feel all messed up in the head. You can tell him a secret and he won't make you feel like a fool.

Bud Light sweepstakes back by the cheese. Paper towels are three rolls for a buck. Do you think somewhere in this world there's another skating rink DJ slash crisis psychotherapist rolling through the grocery store thinking about Jesus and dreams?

Probably not.

"Excuse me," a woman says in a high, singing voice.

"Huh?" I realize I've been lost in thought, rolling side to side in front of women's hygiene.

"Oh, sorry," I tell her. "Waitin' on Brittany's birthday cake."

She reaches across me and holds up a tiny, purple box of pantiliners. "Enjoy it while you're both young," the lady says. "Yesterday I had a baby; now all the sudden she's grown. It goes so fast."

For some reason people tell me things. That probably means something too.

"How 'bout that cookie?" Aunt Piggly asks when I skate back up.

"Best cookie ever," I reply.

"Pretty good, if I do say so myself," she says, handing over the red velvet cake. "Slipped you a couple more inside." She winks and holds a finger to her lips.

"Stay happy," I tell her, reaching over the counter to squeeze her hand. She pulls me to her, wheels off the ground, into a quick embrace. Aunt Piggly hugs exactly like you think she would. Sweet and fluffy, smelling of pies and cake.

The double doors whoosh open and I roll out through the

parking lot, holding Brittany's cake. A wide-eyed tyke with por-cupine hair is being dragged toward the store by his mother.

"Whoa!" he says, spotting me. "You can skate in the grocery store?"

"Sure," I tell him.

"Whoa!" he says. "You're not afraid to drop that cake?"

"No way," I say, spinning backward and holding it over my head.

"Do you know who this is, Charlie?" the mom asks.

I roll back and waggle my skate, anticipating the response. Charlie leans in, checking me out. Doesn't register.

"When Papa Jim got sick, this is the man who helped him get better."

"I did?"

"You did," she says. "You came to the house and talked Daddy into going to rehab. Took him in your truck."

"Is he doing all right?"

"Much better now. You pulled some good magic that night."

"Ah, there's no magic," I tell her. "Just show up and do the best you can. Glad I could help. Someday I might need a ride to rehab, you know?"

"Me and Papa Jim went fishing last Saturday," Charlie says, holding his hands a half foot apart. "And I caught a fish *this* big."

I reach into my pocket and hand him two passes. "Come and see me, my man. I'll teach you how to carry a cake on skates, okay?"

THIRTY MINUTES LATER THE CANDLES ARE LIT AND THE music is loud, children are singing and ten twirling disco balls throw light against the walls. An eight-year-old with silver braces, her hair in cornrows and a tiara that says *Birthday Girl*, rushes over and yanks on my hand.

"You are so awesome!" she yells. "My party rocks!"

After Brittany's bash ends at nine, we drag the moonwalk to the middle of the floor and kick the smoke machines on high. It's Nikki and me and the rest of the rink staff, Jessie and Jenny and Ike. In a roller rink, you are forever thirteen.

A mix list of classic skate songs booms through massive speakers. We wrestle and bounce while a thousand sparkles swarm the fog around us.

"This is *it*," I shout as the sounds of Debbie Deb segue into DJ Kool.

"What is?" asks Jessie, a chesty blonde tomboy. We laugh; me laughing at her laughing at me.

"This is," I tell her.

She jostles me into a headlock then drop-kicks me into the corner. "What are you talkin' about?" Jessie says.

Scaling the moonwalk wall, I backflip over the bunch of them, bounce up, and tell her again. *"This!"*

FOURTEEN

THE KINGDOM IS NOW

*"One of my realizations in such an
earthy atmosphere was that many of the
burning theological issues in the church
were neither burning nor theological."*

–BRENNAN MANNING

TERRY IS THE OTHER PSYCH WARD NIGHT TECH, A LEAN
fellow with sort of a concave chest and belly roll, hairy as a
Sasquatch everywhere, tragically, except for the top of his head,
where only lonesome wisps are scattered about. The patients love
him—even the old rednecks strung out on meth—because he's
so down-to-earth and easy to talk to.

At one time Terry was the music minister at a big church in
town. He loved his job but eventually confessed his struggles to
an associate pastor and asked for help. Gossip spread swiftly and
what was said in confidence was twisted and told throughout the
church. Terry was let go.

He strayed awhile and then started his own support group,
meeting weekly with other outcasts, discussing how difficult it

is not to drink or drug or be promiscuous. I can tell he misses *church* church though. I'm in the break room making chart notes while he cleans.

"Did you go Sunday?" he asks. "Is your praise team doing that 'We Lift Our Hands' song?" His lily-white arms arch to the ceiling, swaying forth and back. "I love that song," he says, squeezing his eyes shut, singing a little run from the chorus. He snaps to, gazing up. "Good gosh, I've got Kermit arms. So what's y'all's summer mission project?"

"I think we're sending the youth to do mime at the Mall of America. How 'bout your group? Still going?"

"Monday nights at Loose Diamonds," he says, dismantling the coffeepot and washing the parts in a tiny sink. "We've been supporting this mission that buys back sex trafficking victims from Thailand, helps them start their own business or get a trade." Terry digs through his wallet and shows me a smiling picture of a brown-skinned girl. "This is Sarai. She's a school-teacher now." He pauses. "Okay, so maybe we don't improve *all* of their lives. But I figure maybe if I help save enough sex-trade slaves God might be a little more gracious with me, you know?"

I'm about to reply when the intercom buzzes. A sheriff's deputy on the closed-circuit screen nudges a man in shackles and a hospital gown.

"Why do they have to handcuff the psych patients?" Terry groans. He stabs the call button and speaks into the panel. "Be right there."

We make our way through three sets of electro-locked steel doors, out to the circle drive.

"Commitment case for you. Felix DeLeon," says the dep-uty, shoving papers into our hands. Bleary, weary, and totally bewildered, DeLeon looks like George Carlin after all-you-can-drink dollar wine night followed by a fist fight in a Dumpster.

"Come on, Mr. Felix," Terry says, guiding him gently by the arm. "You're in good hands now."

The old drunk stumbles, his eyes rolling over the both of us. "And jes who the hel'r you?" he slurs.

"Best of luck, gentlemen," the deputy says as he removes the cuffs. "He's all yours."

We escort Felix to his room and check his luggage: clothes and deodorant stuffed into grocery sacks. Terry finds a Gideon Bible and starts leafing through the pages.

"Listen to this one," he says, clearing his throat. "I tell you the truth, tax collectors and prostitutes are entering the Kingdom of God ahead of you." He slips the Bible back into the bag. "Did you know that in Hebrew, *Kingdom of God* means a present-day reality and not so much later in heaven?" He pulls a pair of grubby loafers from the sack, lifts the insole, and holds up a small baggie filled with pills. "It just means a better way of living right now."

"Aww, man . . .," Felix pants, lolling his head from side to side.

Back in the break room things get quiet. The eleven-to-seven nurse is grazing on microwave popcorn and shuffling through late-night cable in the lounge.

"Where'd you learn Hebrew?" I ask him.

"Bible college," Terry says. "I've always felt called to some sort of ministry. Was thinking of going back to seminary before the church thing fell through. But that all seems a long way away now."

"So they just fired you?"

"No, first they sent me to one of those workshops where they try to reprogram you."

"How'd that work?" I ask.

"Pfff," he scoffs. "Usually just makes things worse."

I laugh but Terry doesn't.

"Serious," he says. "This guy tells his story about how he got delivered, *'Praise the Lord,'* crying and all that. Two weeks later I saw him at Silly Sally's dancing to the Oak Ridge Boys."

"Oak Ridge Boys?"

"It was country night," Terry says, slapping the desk. "Had on a cowboy hat with a purple feather in it. I went up to him like, 'Aren't you Mr. Straight and Narrow now?'"

"That's pretty wild," I reply.

"You know how it is. Liars, adulterers, come on in—but we've got about two visits to get right and change teams." Terry leans against the tech's desk and takes a long deep breath. "I worry sometimes though. What if they're right?" He rustles through the drawer and digs out a pack of saltines. "I don't feel like I chose this . . . Cracker?"

"No thanks," I reply. "Terry, I don't know, man. If it was up to me, church would say: 'Come on in everybody, anybody. We're all praying for God to be patient and help us figure out this crazy life thing. First though, we're going to work on the mean people.'"

"Hallelujah." He laughs, crumbs tumbling from the side of his mouth. "Come on, I need a cigarette."

In the middle of the psych ward courtyard there's the ghost of a swimming pool, filled with concrete after a teenage boy tied himself to a lounge chair and drowned. We walk around the silhouette of the old diving board, not saying much, Terry smoking and me drinking a Diet Coke. Suddenly there's a pull at my shirttail.

"Spot me a smoke, Captain?" Felix says between hacks, his shivering frame bent and frail beneath a thin V-neck tee.

"He don't smoke," Terry snaps playfully. "Here."

With the focus of a man defusing a bomb, Felix slides out a cigarette and cups it between both hands like a delicate baby bird.

"Light?" he begs, interrupted by a tremendous hacking fit. Terry takes Felix's trembling fist and holds their cigarettes together until both ends begin to glow.

"Shanks," says the grizzled old addict, wobbling to the corner of the concrete slab and sitting with his arms across his knees.

"If Felix is gonna make it through detox somebody's gonna need to bring him some friggin' cigarettes," Terry says. He holds his Winston between two fingers and takes a slow drag. "Guess I could pick some up tomorrow on the way in."

"I can do it," I offer.

Terry shakes his head. "I have to stop anyway." He sighs, letting the vapor slip from the side of his mouth. "God knows I might be in a place like this someday and need somebody to be nice to me."

We stand there on the deep end of the psych ward pool, watching Felix in the shallows, flat on his back, blowing smoke to the stars.

"So uh, Terry," I ask. "Do you think you're still called?"

He cranes his head back, staring into the night for a long silent time. A white streak flashes, falling across the sky. Terry traces it with his cigarette and smiles. "Yeah," he says. "Sometimes."

"Maybe," I tell him, "it's not too late."

THE YOUTH PASTOR'S WIFE IS NEARLY TEN MONTHS PREG-
nant with twins. The janitor was going to cover for him but his
gout flared up. So they asked me to lead the young-adult service
on Wednesday night.

Get this: Dean Gage called me to his office a while back,
and I was afraid it might be to boot me out of grad school for my
lack of focus and lackadaisical attitude. But instead he offered
me a teaching assistantship. It's just a lab class, but still. I teach
college now.

So I put together a proper lesson for the Wednesday-night
service, something smart with illustrations and bullet points.
But today it all feels shallow and plastic. As I'm driving to church
a new message starts stirring, and what I really think I need to
talk about is how it seems sometimes God delights in trashing
our plans. Messing with our heads. Kicking religious idols over
and cutting prejudices to shreds.

What I should do is share the story of drunk old Felix and
Terry's call. Do we really believe that love covers a multitude of
sins? That God can use anybody, anywhere? Or was that only
back in the Bible days?

Or maybe I could tell them about Caroline, the agnostic girl
from Canada in my effective listening class who's really insight-
ful, down-to-earth, and volunteers at the homeless shelter two
days a week. You know what she does at the shelter? Whatever
needs to be done. Cooks, cleans, serves food. Clips nails and
checks new residents for lice. What does it say when the non-
believer is a better Christian than me?

Caroline asked me some really interesting questions the
other day: "Why do church people only come in big packs and
van loads? Like once or twice a year maybe? Why do you only

want to preach or hand out religious materials? How come you only talk to each other and not the residents?"

I don't want to deliver a sermon or debate theology or beat anybody up with the Bible. I just want to have an honest conversation about how every time I turn around it seems my preconceived notions about right and wrong get smashed.

If I'm preaching to anybody, it's myself. Because honestly, I haven't always been respectful to those different from me. I've been critical and selfish and mean. I have put my own need to be right ahead of the call to be gracious, to walk out my faith with practical kindness and an attitude tempered with humility and joy. It isn't my job to judge who's got it and who doesn't, who's going to make it and who'll be left behind. That's not grace; it's arrogance and insecurity. Judging is God's business, not mine.

There's a part in the Bible that says the grace I give will be measured back to me the same. That's a scary thought, really. But it makes me want to be kinder and not so quick to throw stones. Self-examination is the higher call. Criticizing and pointing out the faults of others is a low, weak level of religion that only attracts weak-hearted, closed-minded fools. That's why Jesus warned against obsessing over the speck of sawdust in someone else's eye while being oblivious to the whole tree stuck in your own.

By the time I pull into the church parking lot, the message is like fire in my bones. That gout-toed janitor's got nothing on me. The young-adult class that meets in the storeroom above the kitchen on Wednesday nights? I am so ready.

But the room is packed and there are older adults here too. One of the associate pastors has come to keep an eye on things. That hyperactive kid from the praise band has everyone doing the pogo to a song that talks about how Christians should be happy, happy all the, all the time, and someone painted a mural of a big, beautiful Bee Gees Jesus with billowy hair and outstretched hands on the wall behind the pulpit. At the last minute, I lose my nerve and go with the lesson that's safe and plastic. If you want to succeed in church circles it's easier to simply follow the script.

Afterward, everybody says I did fine, but I'm not convinced. There's only one opinion that really matters. I don't think God likes it when we take the easy way out.

I was hoping maybe he'd catch a ride with someone else, but when I get back to the truck Jesus is waiting, leaning against the hood, and writing in the dust with his finger. Whoever does those pictures for church foyers and Christian bookstores is charitable because truth is, in person, he doesn't look like much. If Jesus were a Bee Gee, he'd be Maurice. Except for the eyes. He can say a lot without speaking a word.

"Sorry, Jesus," I explain, avoiding those eyes. "Guess I lost my nerve."

I stand with the door open and one hand on the wheel, the heel of my boot resting against the frame. Traffic streams slowly by. The sign at the bank flashes the temperature and time. Across the street at the Laundromat, an old woman folds her clothes. Jesus nearly smiles, turns, and draws in the dust again.

"C'mon," I tell him, sliding in to start the engine. "Let's go home."

FIFTEEN

JUMBO THIN MINT AND THE JAUNDICED CHIMP

*"But God hath chosen the foolish things
of the world to confound the wise."*

−1 CORINTHIANS 1:27 AKJV

IT'S SOMEWHERE SOUTH OF MIDNIGHT AND I'M WATCHING a TV preacher in a shiny black suit, salmon-colored tie, and a suspiciously robust head of hair for a man his age. He flashes a stunning white smile to the camera, steps down from the platform, and with perfect timing says, "There is nothing in your life easier to replace than a fool."

That one statement is so rich I send the station a ten-dollar bill.

I have a confession. I love Christian television. Not in the snarky, make-fun-of-it way either. I really get something out of it sometimes.

Don't get me wrong; it's not like Christian programming doesn't give the viewer plenty to poke fun at. But if you are kind of introverted and not into the big-group church thing, Christian TV can be a good place to hear quality teaching and preaching. National-level communicators. Top-notch storytellers. If you're truly talented, they just might put you on TV.

Christian networks really aren't that much different than secular ones. It's about 92 percent ridiculous, and every now and then you find something exceptional that inspires you to step up and see the beauty in life—to be a better spouse or parent or neighbor or friend. So why knock that?

THE LOCAL GOSPEL TV STATION ASKS ME TO BE A GUEST. Fascinated by the genre, I cannot resist and am booked for a Tuesday evening in the last hour of a three-hour show.

Before I appear, the musical guests are up—a church group from Albania. A swarthy man with an apple-shaped head plays an instrument, something resembling an end table with a handle on the side. He cranks its handle, and a sound like kazoos in a meat grinder oozes forth while a spooky-eyed woman bangs a sporadic tambourine and atonally sings a three-note chorus for roughly nine minutes.

In the background, a Latino fellow as tall as Shaquille O'Neal is folded into a school desk, hand-drumming on the lid with the sort of facial expressions that might accompany playing through the "Angry Sun" level from *Super Mario Bros. 3.*

They wheeze to a finish as the camera pans to fourteen men in tatty brown suits with high-water pants holding hands and singing "How Great Thou Art" in their native tongue, in unison.

While their last note dies, the show's host, a heavyset man with a mismatched toupee, rallies his fist and says, "Well,

Halle-*lu*-jah!" I'm standing there like I've just seen Father Abraham do the funky chicken when the stage director waves me onto the set.

As I stagger toward the host, trying to come up with an honest opening line to express astonishment without resorting to profanity, a thought rushes into my head that's so loud and alien I know it must be the voice of the Lord.

This is where you will always belong.

"Of course," I tell Jesus. "Great."

The TV lights are hot and too bright. I'm sweating from the heat and nervous energy. In a mint-green jacket with matching tie and black shirt, the show's host reminds me of a supersized Girl Scout cookie. I start to mention this on air but pull back at the last second.

"You know," he brays, "through good times and bad, my life verse has been Romans, eight and twenty-eight: *And we know all things . . . work together. For the good.* Share with us, brother, if you will, *your* life verse."

It's a live, three-hour show, on five nights a week. The host paces slow.

I shift in my seat and scratch behind my neck. "Psalm 2:4: God sits in the heavens and laughs," I tell him.

"Well, glory," he replies. "That is a new one. On me."

"When I die," I say, "God will tell me what he's been laughing at. When he does, I'll laugh too. And everything will finally be all right." There's a bit of dead air. Then I say, "I hope."

The host turns to the camera and carefully repeats my verse, as if viewers might be learning impaired. "Ha, *ha*," he says. "That's an *incredible* impartation. From the Word. What a wonderful, inspired *hope* we have as joint heirs . . . with Christ."

"Sometimes," I add, "I just go ahead and laugh with God now."
There is a ringing silence. The cameraman sneezes. I smile
like a kindergartner on picture day. The girl who cuts my hair
will later say I looked like a jaundiced chimp.

The host sits back and lets his jacket fall open. I can see the
outline of a girdle straining against his shirt. Sweat trickles from
his wig, and there's a bald patch between the fluffy, white sides
and steel-black top. He smiles and nods like no time is passing
at all.

Christians. You understand why some people poke fun. But
it's not like the Bible is a document dedicated to well-balanced
characters. I'm sure Moses seemed pretty out there in his day.
Everybody thought Noah was some nut. David danced half-
naked in the street. Check out that story about how Ezekiel baked
his bread sometime. John the Baptist *and* John the Revelator.
One ate locusts and the other saw seven-headed dragons in the
sky. Some people even thought Jesus had lost his mind. Doesn't
the Bible say God uses the foolish to confound the wise? So who
am I to judge? Maybe this is where I belong.

Finally, the host speaks. "The man who laughs . . . with *God*,
ha *ha*," he says as the High-Water Brothers' Fourteen-Man Quartet
and Shaq and the Spooky Kazoos cluster together on the catty-
corner set for one last rousing song. The host points to me and
asks, "Now, brother. Are you ready . . . to get abundantly—*blessed*?"

"Oh, yes," I reply.

SIXTEEN

THIS IS THE MATTRESS TRICK

"It seems strange to think that turning yourself over to your own bewilderment would actually bring clarity, but it does. Solving this riddle is the beginning of any true spiritual journey."

–ANDREW W. K.

A NINETEEN-YEAR-OLD PATIENT WITH FROSTED TIPS AND a tight, Lycra tee smuggled in a steak knife and is barricaded in the bathroom, threatening to stab himself in the heart.

There are so many patients and so little staff; I don't really know him. Dual diagnosis. Depression. Addiction to OxyContin maybe. Moody, histrionic at times. Manipulative. I might be thinking of the wrong guy.

The psych ward bathrooms are Jack and Jill, so I enter from the opposite side, hands up and moving slow. Now I know this guy. Dark, deep-set eyes. Hair razored on the sides and long on top. Walks as close as he can to the walls with his head down, like a beaten dog. Moody, manipulative—he's the one.

"Easy," I say in my softest voice. "We're only here to help."

There are two more techs behind me, a new kid and Heather—
the star college athlete we nicknamed Softball.

"Sick of this place. *Sick of it*," David shouts.

Softball had ordered him to end his call just as phone times
were over. He was already set off, and things escalated from there
until he stormed down the hall and slammed his door. The knife
is in his right hand, upside down from the way you'd cut a steak.
He isn't pointing it at me or at himself. I edge in.

"I know, I know. This place sucks," I tell him. "Look, I'm not
telling you what you can or can't do. If you really want to hurt
yourself there's nothing I can do to stop you."

"That's right," David says.

"Right," I affirm, taking another step closer. He's sitting sideways between the tub and toilet. The knife hand lowers and rests
by his leg now. "Just talk to me a minute so I can say I tried, man,
please." My heart is breaking and it shows in my face. I say it again.
"David, please."

"You can talk," he says. "But tell her to get back." I look over
and see Softball's face in the door.

"Phone time was *over*, David," she says. "You don't get special privileges."

"Shut up, bulldog!" he says. "Take your ugly face on home!"
In a comically tragic moment, he yanks the toilet paper from
the holder and lobs it pathetically at her with his left hand.

Softball ducks and pops back in, the new tech's eyes wide
over her shoulder.

"David," she warns. "You better chill, man."

"Whoa. Whoa," I say in my calmest voice. "Everybody cool
out. We're fine. Y'all step on back. Me and Mr. David are just
gonna talk here."

Softball shoots David a steely glare.

"Heather, go on," I scold. "Sit over there on the *bed* and ratchet yourself down some. Geez."

David breathes heavy, his nostrils flaring like an angry bull's. The knife hand twitches, higher now.

"David, you're not going to try to stab me, are you?" He shakes his head no.

"It's just us," I tell him. "Whatever you wanna talk about, I'll hear you out and help best I can. Okay if I sit over here?"

"I don't care," he says. Then louder, so Softball can hear. "Sick of *some* people in my space all the time, telling me what to do! Sick of this place, sick of these pills, sick of all this!" He sets the knife against his wrist until the blade creases the skin.

"Slow down. Slow, easy," I tell him, easing myself onto the edge of the tub with a wince. "*Agh.* Sorry. Screwed my knee up playing volleyball in the gym last night. Ol' Wes Express jumped high for the slam and—" I reach toward the ceiling and slap the wall hard as I can.

David flinches, looking toward the slap as Softball storms in from the other door, flattening him with a thin mattress while I step on his right wrist. He tries to pull away but I lean my weight against his arm until he drops the knife.

Softball pitches the mattress and knife to the side, straddling David, her knees on his shoulders, her hard face close and tight. "You really think we're gonna let you stab yourself?" she growls. "This is the mattress trick."

David looks past her to me, hurt and confusion over his face. "You lied?" he asks in a pitiful tone.

"Of course I lied." I pick up the blade and turn it in the light. "Wouldn't you?"

"No," he says defiantly. Thrashing, he catches Softball by surprise but is no match for her superior strength. She pins him back to the floor; he acts as if he's about to spit in her face. I reach over and rake my knuckles across his sternum until he yelps and goes limp.

"David, please," I say. "Be cool."

The new tech returns with the nurse. "Already got the order. Put him in the restraints," she says, before they head off toward a new set of screams ringing down the hall.

"What kind of hellhole is this?" David cries.

"It sure ain't Disney," I confess. Then in the calm voice again, "Look, I'm sorry, but we had to get the knife. Everything's safe now. We don't have to do restraints. We'll sit with you in seclusion. I'll listen as long as you want to talk. It's your choice."

The sink hangs crooked from the previous patient's midnight tryst and there's a bottle of White Rain shampoo spilled out in the corner of the floor. With a whimper, David turns to the wall.

Softball sits back, off his shoulders. "I'm sorry too," she says, taking his chin and pulling his face back to us. "Just doing my job." Then, after a while, "But I understand more than you know. I was a patient here. I've been right where you are. Mattress trick and all."

He looks to me for confirmation and I nod. "They lock you up in here too?" he asks.

"Not yet," I tell him. "But tomorrow's another day."

David lays his head back against the tile floor, staring at the lights, wondering, I imagine, how life came to this. His face changes, lighter, like he's in on the joke.

"Put me in the restraints," he says.

"You sure?" Softball asks.

"Yes," he says.

We lift him up and he rides limp against us, his arms across our shoulders, feet dragging behind.

Seclusion is the last room down the hall. A ten-by-ten cell with soft pink cinderblock walls and a hospital bed in the middle of the floor. The carpet is low pile, stained by blood and sweat and snot and tears, and the electrical sockets have all been removed. There's a camera in the corner protected by Plexiglas and a window that's half covered by a sheet on the far wall.

We lay David on the bed and fasten the straps: wrists and ankles, another across the chest. Softball pulls a blanket over him, tucking it under his shoulders and hips.

"You okay?" I ask.

"Yes," he says. "I'm all right."

"You want me or Softball to stay with you?"

A look passes between them, something familiar I can't quite place. He softly says, "Let Heather stay."

I slip out, glancing through the observation glass before I walk away. Their faces are close, talking. Heather nods. It's strange how in the psych ward you can be enemies one minute and allies the next. But really, that's kind of my favorite part.

Heather wets a washcloth and wipes David's face, and that's when he begins to cry. She reaches over and takes his hand.

"Jamie," the new tech calls from down the hall.

I turn to him. "Yeah?"

"Hurry," he says, pointing toward more screams. "Come on."

ON THE WAY HOME, I STOP AT THE ALL-NIGHT GROCERY for cereal and eggs. Late-night grocery stores always feel like church to me, like there's a holy loneliness in the waxed lino-leum, the ordered peace of stacked bags of charcoal and walls of canned peas. An old *Super Zaxxon* machine is wedged between the magazines and produce. I waste a few quarters just to escape awhile.

A stocker passes. He has long graying hair, a gnarled arm, and is pushing a dust mop with his good hand.

"You get past a million, let me know," he says. "I'll play ya on break."

"You got it," I tell him. "Broke a million, huh?"

He leans over and taps the screen. "See that high score? KKX? That's me."

"What's KKX stand for?"

"Kick-axe," he brags, pumping his good fist.

"Nice to meet you, Mr. Kick-Axe," I say as he pushes his mop away. Then, as he turns down the first row. "When I hit a mil, I'm comin' for you . . . ." Somewhere over the salsa, I hear him laugh.

Near the cantaloupes, there's a stack of composition note-books, fifty-nine cents apiece. I buy two, take my Cocoa Pebbles home, and start writing about all the funny, nutty, sad, beau-tiful people God brings my way. Nothing fancy, no big agenda, just trying to capture snapshots of those small moments when our stories intersect. Everybody's story matters, I believe. Plus, I see some really amazing stuff and it'd be a crime not to write it down.

As the stories unfold, I say small prayers for peace and guidance for those whose paths I cross. Prayers tonight for David. Prayers for Heather. Prayers for Mr. Kick-Axe with the gnarled arm.

SEVENTEEN

THE EPIPHANY OF THE HOLY AND OF THE ABSURD

"Praise him with loud clashing cymbals!"

–PSALM 150:5 ESV

NURSE SQUIGGLY CALLS WITH A DISPATCH TO A TRAILER park on the outskirts of town. History of schizophrenia, mania, depression, anxiety. The patient's mother called asking for help.

I don't feel like going, don't feel like talking, don't feel like listening. I want to stay home, lie on the floor, and read trash or theology or trashy theology. Watch some stupid movie, grind out Sabbath riffs on my electric guitar. Stay in my own world. I hope whoever it is gets some assistance, but I'd really rather not be involved.

"Squig, why does it always have to be some trailer on the low-rent side of town?" I ask.

"Because that's our people?" she replies.

I call and the lady sounds nice and sort of desperate and worried about her son. I make good money when I leave the house, and there's this gadget I want. If I go, I can rationalize buying it. So I grumble and tell her, "Sure, I'll be right over."

When I pull up to the trailer, the front door is open and the mother waves me inside. "Watch that bottom step, honey," she says from the door frame. "It's loose."

The mother is short and spunky in a flowery housecoat with silver showing through the roots of her squirrel-brown hair.

"I'm Larry's mama," she says.

"Nice to meet you, ma'am."

"Can I get you somethin' to drink?" she asks. "Just made a fresh batch of tea."

"No, thank you." I give the place a quick look around. Cream-colored sofa covered with a sheet. Console television. Dog. Dusty old family photos. "Footprints in the Sand" plaque.

"So, your son is here?"

"Baby!" she hollers down the hall. "The man's here to see you."

"Larry, he's a good boy, just got troubles in the head. Doctor says it's that schizo-free-nia," she tells me, poking at the big black lab sprawled across the couch. "That's Rufus. Don't pay him no mind. Thinks he runs the place." Rufus raises his head and regards me briefly, apparently unimpressed.

Larry appears looking a bit rumpled, a dirty, white apron tied around his waist.

"Aw, man, you didn't have to drive all the way out here. Mama offer you some tea or somethin'?"

"I'm good," I say. "Just come out to see what we could do to help."

"Well thank you, man. You mind talkin' back here?"

I follow Larry down the narrow hall. He's a big dude with a walrus mustache, hair balding up front and long in the back. Smells like bourbon and fajita steam.

"You been drinkin'?" I ask.

"Drinking? Oh. Naw, I'm a cook over to the Bok Bok Wok. That new Chinese place they built next to the dollar store? Just got off. Helps to work but with my mind spinning, it's been hard. Come on, we can talk in here."

Larry flicks on the light to a room not much wider than a walk-in closet. There's a twin bed and old turntable stereo on a shelf. And taking up every other conceivable space in the room, a massive set of Slingerland drums.

"Whoa," I say. "That is one awesome drum set."

"Thanks, man," says Larry. He sits on the drum stool and points to a tapestry of the Rush logo draped over his window to block out the sun. "Rock and roll," he says, nodding his head. "Gets me through."

I edge past the crash cymbals and roto-toms and take a seat on the edge of the bed. Two rosaries are wrapped around the bedpost and a crucifix hangs on the wall above.

"Seems every Rush fan I know is Catholic," I tell Larry. "I grew up Catholic, some."

Larry leans over and clicks on an oscillating fan. "Yeah, me too," he says, turning to look at the cross. "Guess I never thought about it that way."

"Hey, you got your meds here?"

Larry reaches down, pulls a plastic baggie from beneath the pillow in the bass drum and hands it to me. He fidgets while I look the medicine over, clops the bass pedal a few times, and apologizes. "Them pills, I'm not sure they even work no more."

I roll the bottles, noting the doses and drug names. "You still taking these?"

"Yeah, but my ADD gets cranking and I'm—" He waffles his hand and raises it to the ceiling. "Can't concentrate, ain't sleeping. I don't wanna hurt myself or nothin'. My medicines need changing but you know a poor boy can't get no appointment. They said the first one was, like, three months out."

I'm listening and making a few notes, mostly staring over his shoulder at a twenty-plus-piece drum set. Larry swivels to the side and starts softly sizzling the hi-hat open and closed.

"Go on," I tell him. "Cook it."

"You a drummer?" he says.

"Used to be, but . . ." I gesture to the set in a way that says, *Nothing like this, buddy.*

"Wanna hear something?" he says.

"Absolutely," I reply.

Larry mutters to himself a bit and counts in to the incredibly difficult drum solo from "YYZ." Eyes shut, arms flailing, the big man plays like an octopus possessed, attacking the algebraic jazz-rock rhythms of the legendary Neil Peart, peppering the piece with his own abstract improvisations. In the close confines of the single-wide, fills, flams, and paradiddles ricochet from every wall, at times sounding like a boxcar full of firewood falling down a mountain, an armory of machine guns misfiring at once, like the Apocalypse led by the drum corps from a million marching bands. If Saint Irenaeus is right and the glory of God is a man fully alive, then the Almighty has one fist lifted, chanting *"LARRY, LARRY, LARRY!"*

As quickly as he began, he ends, folds his sticks, and gives me a sheepish grin. I sit back slack-jawed. Rufus barks once from down the hall.

"That was insane!" I say, realizing too late that *insane* might not be the most appropriate word. "Dude, why aren't you in a band?"

"Ah, I ain't got nobody to play with," Larry says, wiping the sweat from his neck. "I just play with these old records." There's some gray coming in near his temples and a jagged scar under his eye. He reminds me of Ben Franklin, if Franklin had been in Skynyrd, with a little bit of David Crosby mixed in.

Behind some wadded-up clothes and a fishing pole, there's a classical guitar propped in his closet. I pick it up but it's sorely out of tune.

"Been trying to learn that thing," he says. "It's tough though. You play?"

"Some," I reply, twisting the tuning pegs into place.

"How 'bout *Moving Pictures*, man?" Larry says, holding up Rush's most famous release. "Never be another."

"I hope there is," I say.

"Wouldn't that be cool?" he asks, his words faster and talking with his hands now. "If the band went back in and made seven new songs that fit in right where that one left off. They could call it *More Pictures* or somethin' like that. I know you think I'm nuts now. That's my problem. I'll sit around all day thinking about pointless stuff and not ever get nothin' done. Thank God, Mama's been real good to me."

"Tell you a secret?" I say.

"Yeah, man."

"I think that way a lot too."

"Really?" Larry says. "What do you do to stay straight?"

"Come hang out with people like you."

Larry gives me that sweet, sheepish grin again. "That's cool, brother," he says, shaking his head. I give the tuner one last twist and pluck out the harmonics that begin "Red Barchetta."

"Aw, I know that one," Larry says, just before he joins in on the ride. "Good one."

Call me overspiritual if you wish, or oversensitive, or given to magical thinking or allegorically clumsy or maybe even touched with a bit of psychosis myself. But I'm telling you, somewhere near the middle of the song, God walks into the room. *He must be hovering though,* I think. *Because with all the drums and guitars and octopus arms, there's sure no place to stand.*

"Watch your elbow, Lord," I sing with the warble exclusive to Geddy Lee.

As we fade down the coda, Larry's mom knocks on the door and sticks her head in. She looks at us and smiles, relieved. "You sure you boys don't want some tea or something?"

"Yes ma'am," I tell her. "I'll take a glass."

"Larry, you want some, baby?"

"Yes ma'am," he replies.

She brings in a tray, heavy old glasses with diamond shapes down the side, wrapped in napkins to keep the cold off our hands.

"Say," Larry says, after the first big gulp. "You don't know 'By-Tor and the Snow Dog,' do you?"

Occasionally I get the epiphany, that slim instant when I see the scene removed from myself and realize how ridiculous and perfect it is for a misfit life like mine. The epiphany of the holy, and of the absurd. That God still shows up in unexpected places.

I wish I could cut around the edges and take this moment with me, show it to the people I love who do not understand.

"Don't know it," I reply.

"How about 'La Villa Strangiato'? It's got that classical part at the start."

I laugh, the sort of self-deprecating laugh a man might laugh were he asked to conquer Kilimanjaro on a pogo stick.

"Brother, I'm no Alex Lifeson," I tell him. "But if you start I'll jump in on the middle part."

Larry grabs his sticks and looks the drums over like a road map. His mother makes a face like *Let me get gone,* but first reaches over and squeezes my hand.

"Hey Larry," I say while she's still listening. "I'm gonna get you an appointment this week about your meds. We'll get you fixed up, okay?"

"Sounds good," he says, still scanning drums.

"Sure glad you could come out tonight," says Larry's mom.

"Me too," I tell her.

As Larry clicks his sticks seven times, she trots off down the hall.

EIGHTEEN
WALK ON WATER

"All things are possible after midnight."

–UNKNOWN

THEY CALL THEM THE SMALL HOURS OF THE NIGHT, BUT that isn't true. The hours of the night are spacious and filled with wonder, with restless questions and longings and dreams. The crisis line rings.

"Mister," the caller says in a sad and frantic voice. "You gots to help me."

"I'll try," I tell her. "What's going on?"

"It's my brother, Diego," she says. "He done gone crazy. He's been goin' out to the railroad bridge, saying he's gonna jump. Says he's tired of all this. He's out there right now."

"I can send the police."

"Please don't send no cops. That just makes it worse. Diego, he got priors. He don't need to go to jail. He needs help. Maybe he'll talk to you."

"Give me his number."

It always feels intrusive to call people out of the blue. *Whatever. Just dial.*

"Diego, it's J.," I say. "Suzi sent me. She's worried about you."

"Yeah, man. I'm out here," Diego admits. "Just watching the river roll. Thinking about everything that's messed up. I can't pay my bills. I got a little son but his mama won't let me see him. I been through a lot lately. Sometimes I just don't wanna feel this way no more."

"But you're not going to jump, right?" I ask. To tell the truth, I'm on autopilot, half-listening and distracted, an old rerun of *Soul Train* in the corner of my eye.

"I don't think so tonight. I try to think about Mario. But it's hard, man. It's hard."

After we hang up, Diego stays on my mind. I feel guilty, like I am a rotten crisis-call person, too selfish and inept, never doing enough. The stakes are kind of high, you know? The railroad bridge has been a haunt of mine since the early college days. Lights on the water, slow trains passing in the night. That black, muddy river that flows on to the sea. I drive over and walk the middle rail.

"Hey man. I'm here," I tell Diego from my cell. "On the bridge."

"I'm home now, brother," he says. "Drinking a beer and watching a movie. I think I'll be all right tonight."

"Okay," I tell him. "Call if you need to."

"I will," he says, then with concern, as if our roles have been reversed. "Be careful out there."

There's a platform that juts out over the water and a steel set of stairs that lead to the apex of the frame. From the top of these stairs, you can see the night turn purple in the hour before dawn. It is the most spacious hour of the night.

"Don't worry," I tell Diego. "I will."

IT'S SUNDAY EVENING, AND I AM DRESSED IN A ROBE AND sandals to play Jesus in the church Easter play. I'm more of a back-pew person now, slipping in late and leaving early most Sundays. It makes me feel better to be in a room with all the people. Sometimes, when everyone closes their eyes and sings an old song without the music, I almost feel like I could float through the ceiling back to heaven. I'm pretty sure they picked me to play Jesus because I'm the only guy in church with a beard and long hair.

We draw a large crowd, but I play a dark-eyed Christ—a man of sorrows who often retreats to lonely places. After the production I hang around down at the altar like Pastor Reddy asked. I stand there with my hands clasped before me, waiting, but the congregation passes with eyes lowered or looking away.

I'm backstage about to scrub off my mascara when the pastor leads a young mother into the room. She's holding a little girl wearing a polka-dot dress and white sneakers—a pale, rickety child with straw-yellow hair, her eyes wet with tears.

"What's the matter?" I ask the mom, who is crying too.

"Said she wasn't leaving until she saw Jesus."

The mother sets the little girl down and she stands there, wobbling and sniffling with her hands half covering her face. We look at each other awhile. I can't think of anything else to do, so I stoop down and hold out my hands. She runs over to me, throwing her arms around my neck. Her mother writes on the back of her checkbook and holds it where I can see. In blue ink: *Sadie.*

"Sadie, thank you for coming to see me," I tell her.

Sadie leans back and stares into my eyes. I'm a little afraid of what she might see but I hold her gaze. She pats at my beard and tugs lightly at a handful of hair. "I love you," Sadie says.

I was going to explain that I'm only playing a part, that I'm not really Jesus, that I'm just some long-haired dude who sits in the back of church. But her words are pure and free from doubt and fear. So instead I tell her, "Sadie, I love you too."

Her green eyes are wide now. "You do?" she asks. "Really?"

"Yep," I tell her. "I really do."

There's a big chip in her top front tooth and the tiniest laugh escapes. "Yay," says Sadie, clapping her hands.

Sadie's mom beams when I hand her back, still wiping tears from the corner of her eye. Sadie turns and waves as they walk away. The pastor has been watching from the door. "That's a pretty good Jesus right there," he says.

"Me or Sadie?"

"I guess when we do it right," Reddy says, "everybody gets to be Jesus for a while."

I make my way down the long dark hall to the back of the church, past the glowing green exit sign, and out the door to my truck. On the ride home I think about Sadie and how we're supposed to show up and be Jesus to each other, going the extra mile, walking in kindness and love. I think about Diego, sitting on the railroad bridge, trying hard to hold on.

"The thought of leaving," he had told me on the phone, "sometimes it's all that gets me through. I could jump or lay down for the train. Either way, no more pain."

I wonder if he's out there tonight. I've got jeans on under the Jesus robe. *If you want it to be,* I pray, *let it be.*

I turn the truck around and drive to the bridge. Park, adjust the robe, and walk out over the water. When the wind blows, I hold out my arms, palms up. Because I'm sort of dramatic that way. Besides, how many times do you get to walk the railroad bridge at night dressed like Jesus?

At the midpoint, there's a landing that extends out over the pillars—a short, metal porch with wire rails. It's the best place to look out over the river. Diego is not here. I pull off the robe, walk back, and toss it on the passenger seat. Just as I am about to drive away, a white pickup pulls into the lot across the street.

In the shadows of the cab, I see a barrel-chested man with thick, black hair. He gets out of the truck and walks quickly toward the bridge. I roll the window down.

"Diego," I call.

"How you know my name?" His voice is angry and confused, and I don't know what to say next. "You know me?" he asks at the curb.

"It's me, man," I tell him. "Jamie."

His eyes flitter and then he slumps. "Why are you here?"

"Why are you?" I ask.

"I don't know," he says, the anger drained from his voice now. "I just need to sit."

"Mind if I sit with you?" I ask.

An hour later, we're on the wire rails, feet hanging over the water. "I wish Jesus would just step through the sky right now," Diego says. "And be like, 'Here I am. And here's the plan.'"

"Yeah," I tell him. "I wish that too."

It's nearly midnight on a Sunday, the magical hour when the

street lights sparkle and the air seems infused with the laughing gas of God. While the city sleeps and dreads Monday morning, we watch and wait for the sky to part. After a while, Diego says, "I guess the Lord, he don't always show up the way we want, does he?"

"Guess not," I reply.

A sparrow swoops over and rests on the highest rail. Diego clears his throat, "Can I ask you something, man?" he says in a serious voice.

"Sure," I tell him.

"Don't take this the wrong way," he says.

"Shoot."

"Are you wearing makeup?"

"I was, uh, Jesus in the church play tonight."

"For real?" he says.

"Yeah. Right before I came here."

He smiles first. Then he laughs. "God, man. He's got some mysterious ways, huh?"

Stars are on the water as the sweet old world turns slow. Diego and I, we both laugh. Then we sit and watch, saying nothing at all.

NINETEEN

CRAZY, MESSY THINGS

"I form the light and create darkness,
I make peace and create calamity; I,
the LORD, do all these things."

–ISAIAH 45:7 NKJV

WEDNESDAY: 6:45 P.M.

PASSING THROUGH PICU, I UNWITTINGLY ENTER Armageddon.

A bipolar, barrel-shaped man with short arms and pork-chop sideburns thinks he is the Lord God. Across the room, a slim, floridly psychotic fellow with slicked-back hair and a faded old suede jacket is certain he is Satan himself.

I step between them just as the war to end all wars is about to begin.

"Gentlemen," I say, "Y'all calm down."

Pork Chop Almighty laughs the hyena-on-helium snicker so familiar to psychiatric intensive care.

"This is my beloved son," he says, holding forth his stubby arms to me. "In whom I am well pleased."

Suede Satan snatches up a folding chair and smashes it across the side of my head, sort of like a cowboy movie without the gimmicked wood.

Pork Chop attacks his nemesis in my defense. I stumble and pull him away.

"Not again!" he shouts at the devil. "Lightning on you! Lightning!"

Satan takes a seat at the card table and seems passive now. I hustle Pork Chop into the nearby seclusion room and lock him in. He presses his hand against the window in the door. "I love you with an everlasting love," he calls as I stagger back and lean against the wall.

"Sorry 'bout that," Satan says casually, as he unwraps a package of cheese crackers. "You ain't really his son, is you?"

"No sir," I reply.

The psychopathic Prince of Darkness nods, bites off half a cracker, and fumbles with a container of chocolate milk. "Hey, can you open this for me?" he asks.

A trickle of blood seeps down the side of my neck. "Sure," I say. I tear open the spout and hand it back. His eyes are lifeless, focused on the void. If Suede Satan stands, I've already got it planned. I'll pin his arms and take him down hard, clipping his skull on the table as we fall. It'll look like an accident.

He takes a long drink, folds closed the spout, and places the milk back on the table. "Thank you," he says.

Jackie, the charge nurse, drags her oxygen tank back in from the smoking porch and takes a quick look around. Two psychotic patients, one in seclusion, broken chair, psych tech with glassy eyes.

"Sit down, Jamie," she says to me with the seen-it-all glaze of a thirty-year career psych nurse. "You dizzy?"

"Little bit."

She fills a bag with ice and presses it above my ear. "You ever had any concussions before?"

"A few," I tell her.

"How many?"

"When I was seven I got busted in the head with a baseball bat. Knocked me out cold. The doc said they'd be easier to get after that. Three or four since then. Five, maybe."

Jackie takes a book down from the nurses' station shelf, flips to a page, and reads, "Symptoms of multiple concussions: Mood swings, restlessness, trouble concentrating, bothered by bright lights, trouble expressing thoughts or finding the right words. Confusion."

"Hon, you ever have any of them symptoms?" Jackie asks.

"A few," I confess.

Pork Chop taps on the glass until Satan turns to look. With that weasel laugh, Porky cries, "Lightning on you!"

Suede Satan stands and hurls his milk carton into the seclusion room glass. Chocolate splatters, running down the pane. It drips to the floor as Pork Chop dances, fire in his eyes. He throws forth his fat little hands and shouts again.

"Lightning!"

"Crazy ol' psych patients." Jackie sighs. "Don't you just love 'em?"

8:05 P.M.

A crew-cut mechanic with first-onset psychosis puts his foot through the lounge television, screaming, "Lee Greenwood is the Whore of Babylon!" He gives us a fight but we get the needle in, ten milligrams of Haldol/ Ativan/ Benadryl, and within minutes he's a sweetheart again.

"Heard a lot of end-times prophecies," I say, "but never anything about Lee Greenwood."

A one-legged OxyContin fiend in American-flag pajamas shakes her juice box at me and says, "That fool's been flipping back and forth between CMT and TBN all night. I tried to tell y'all some bull like this was gonna go down."

"Sorry," I tell her.

She slurps out the last of her juice box and shoots me a beady glare. "Sorry?" she says. "What good is that? Are you gonna get me a new TV or what?"

8:30 P.M.

A female patient with Einstein's hair and the physique of a Green Bay lineman wriggles free from my waist lock and sinks her teeth into my jeans, just to the right of the zipper. Thank God for baggy pants.

When we stick her, she roars like a grizzly and sinks to the floor. Before I leave, she calls me over and says in the sweetest voice that I look *just* like her son, Marlon. She takes me by the hand and sings the first verse of "You Light Up My Life."

9:09 P.M.

I'm knocking on doors down adolescent hall. "Med time," I say.

Teenage patients shuffle to the nurses' station in gym shorts, oversized tees, and bunny slippers. Two are missing. Second to last door on the right.

"Med time," I call, knocking at their door. I wait, listen, and knock again. "Let's go, girls."

"Come in," a muffled voice says.

"Let's go," I say through the door. "C'mon, get your meds."

"I need some help in here," a tiny voice returns.

Everyone is down at the station. I open the door. Both girls are naked from the waist up, posing with hands on their hips. The curly-headed girl half-covers herself with one hand and gives me a fake look of surprise. The straight-haired brunette just smiles. I'm frozen, caught in their trap.

"We want cigarettes," Straight Brunette says with a flirty smirk. "Or we're tellin'."

Bluff. Think quick. "Ladies, please," I say dismissively. "It's like, flash your chest for cigarettes every other day in this place."

"Told you, Sondra," Curly Girl says with disgust as she pulls on her shirt. "Told you he wouldn't give us no cigarettes. We shoulda tried that other guy."

Sondra is still smirking, shirtless, and staring straight into my eyes. "What's your *problem*?" she asks.

9:45 P.M.

There's a call to the front, a new patient coming from the local ER. "This one's pretty bad off," the lady cop says. "Blood-alcohol level of .36, stitches in her wrist."

It's the lead therapist from when I first started, sitting shackled in the backseat. She was a good counselor who cared about people and tried really hard to go the extra mile. Maybe too hard. Late nights and early mornings, weekends on call. Liza was here all the time, always putting out fires, always in the middle of someone's pain. Then one day she was gone. I thought maybe she just found a better job.

"C'mon, hon," the officer says, easing her from the car and helping her to stand. "We're here."

My old coworker is a shell of herself; disoriented, disheveled, her hair knotted and grey. She looks old and exhausted and I can tell she is far from herself, lost in some dark and awful place. For a foggy minute she doesn't recognize me, then the tiniest of lights flickers in her eyes.

"Thank God it's you," Liza cries, collapsing against me. "I am so ashamed."

I stand with arms around her and let her cry, shoulders heaving, wracked with sobs. Part of me wants to console her and promise it'll be all right, but another part has one eye on the narrow drive that leads back to the highway because I want to get as far as possible from this kind of pain. But if I were to break away, dash to my truck, and cut tracks down the driveway, well, I'd probably get fired. Plus, it would be a really rotten thing to do. So I stand with arms around her while she cries, until finally I step back and say, "Come on, Miss Liza. We have to go inside."

I walk her through the double doors and down the back hall, her eyes on the floor and arms clinging to my elbow. The unit is pretty much vacant, thank God. Near the nurses' station she stops and stares at an office across the way.

"I used to work right there . . .," she says, in a voice so far away and fractured it's like an international phone call from Iceland, 1935.

I detour to the smoking porch and pass her the lighter. She

sits and stares at it for the longest time before finally lighting up. Neither of us speaks. She draws deep and looks me over.

"Mercy, Jamie," she mutters. "What happened to you?"

I step in front of the porch window. With the office lights off it reflects back like a mirror. Shirt torn, bandage around my head, plaster scattered in my hair. Blood on my arm and neck, glazed look in my eyes. Seems I've lost a shoe.

"What are you talking about?" I ask. "Is my hair messed up or something?"

Another long puff. Shakes her head. "What happened to your shoes?"

"Shoes?" I say, clueless.

"Tried to tell you," she says, zoning out again.

Before I can reply, the loudspeaker crackles to life: "Dr. Strong. ADU."

"Stay here," I tell her. "I'll be right back."

10:05 P.M.

"Dr. Strong. ADU!"

One hall over, Johnny Ray is slapping out lightbulbs and tearing fixtures off the wall.

The nurse runs for her Thorazine while I wrestle Johnny Ray toward the seclusion room. At the door he trips and we both go tumbling. The back of my head smacks the floor and Johnny catches the carpet hard.

I roll to the side, one hand clutching my head. Johnny Ray crawls to the corner, lip smashed and a nasty scrape rising below his eye.

"Just go on," he says, choking back tears. "Do whatever it is y'all got to do."

I pick up a chair and heave it into the wall. The legs stick; it juts out sideways from the berm. He tucks his head between his knees as I slide down beside him.

"Let it on out," Johnny says slowly, his hollow face tilted, a filmy set of teeth poking over his bloody lip. "Don't do no good to keep it all in."

For seven long seconds, the world is still. The door cracks open. Liza slips in and sits between us, one hand in Johnny's, the other in mine.

"Just breathe," she says. "It'll be all right."

IT'S LATE BY THE TIME I GET BACK HOME. I'D BEEN LIVING in a cracker-box apartment by the college, struggling to get by, but I just moved into a poolhouse. Actually, it's pretty nice. A Graceland-era colonial Gothic on the old-money side of town. Secret gardens, a grotto with a lagoon. The owner is an eccentric playwright from New York. I hear Warhol once swam in the pool. Capote too. Hundred bucks a month, all bills paid, and all I have to do is watch after the estate. Mostly, I've got it to myself.

The path to the levee is two streets over on Sweet Olive Lane. A dark ribbon of asphalt that threads between old Southern mansions and the slow-moving waters of Bayou Cachette. I slip my bicycle out just to ride awhile and clear my mind, letting thoughts run free.

I hope God kept a video of that time Jesus got mad and made a whip. When I get to heaven, I want to see that one. I want to see that ordeal with the fig tree too. And the time he got fed up with the disciples and asked basically, "How long do I have to put up with these guys?" I like those parts in the Bible where Jesus gets mad or rolls his eyes. That part that says he was 100 percent divine and still walked everywhere and got frustrated and tired. Those difficult parts don't hurt my faith. They help. It's good to know God is willing to get in the middle of messy situations. If I were Jesus I probably would have waited to come to earth until there were jet airplanes and Christian TV. Either that, or I never would have left the carpenter's shop.

The streets are vacant and lights in the houses are dim. There's only the sound of tires on pavement and the teeth of the bike chain slowly clinking. An Australian shepherd with charcoal fur and one white stripe dashes from a side yard to run beside me, not barking, just keeping pace. I pedal slow and coast so she can tag along. Just before the long curve she breaks away, vanishing into the trees.

I used to think if a person wanted to be Christlike, they had to have the right responses all the time. To be profound and prudent and spiritually astute. Serious, busy, and sure. I never could pull it off. Not even close.

But Jesus said, "My burden is light." I have to remind myself of that a lot. In the Gospels, Jesus took a pretty easy pace. He didn't even start ministry until he was thirty. When the disciples got all anxious and pushy, he didn't let that bother him much. If the gospel is all about pushing and producing, Jesus was pretty inefficient in his time. If "seriously busy and sure" was our standard, we'd be singing hymns about Judas instead of Jesus Christ.

Since I've been at the hospital, I'm finding that people generally don't care how profound or spiritually productive you are. Thank God it isn't that hard. Just show up and be real. Let the person who is hurting take the conversation wherever they need it to go. Be willing to listen or laugh or admit something is sad and awful without a bunch of phony answers or advice. Jesus didn't browbeat or patronize. He just showed up, willing to get his hands dirty, willing to get in the middle of crazy, messy things.

So maybe that means I'm not doing so bad after all. I don't know. I'll feel one thing tonight and something else tomorrow. If Jesus is the good teacher, I don't think I'm quite ready for his gifted class. *Do you have a remedial class, Jesus? You know, for people like me?*

But all those thoughts begin to fade as I weave through the sprinklers near the end of the lane. The road goes on beyond the dead-end sign, if you know the hidden way. Up a narrow dirt path and down the levee to a spot where the bayou flows into the river, the oak trees break away, and God walks in the cool of the night.

Drift boats pass slow and you can sit and watch the moon sail across the stars as the river laps over the shore. I stay until blue creeps into the edges of the night sky, listening to God listen, watching him watch.

By sunrise I am sleeping the easy, dreamless sleep of peace.

TWENTY

JUST ONE SIGN

"The Lord *is close to the brokenhearted;*
he saves those whose spirits are crushed."

—PSALM 34:18 CEB

ROLLER RINK FRIDAY AND SATURDAY NIGHTS. BLACKLIGHTS
and birthday cakes, limbo rock and couples only, fog machines and
thumping bass, the smell of hot popcorn and dirty shoes.

"This Diet Coke tastes like feet," I tell Mr. Ric.

"Tastes fine to me," he says, taking a sip of his own. "Listen,
we're really getting busy on parties lately. You want to come help
out Saturday afternoons too?"

I've got a graduate assistantship, I work part time at the psych
ward, and I carry crisis calls at night. But poor college students
need all the extra cash they can get. Besides, the rink is a blast and
it keeps me sane.

"Yeah," I reply. "Absolutely."

I'm driving reckless on the interstate back home, blaring the
Misfits' "We Are 138." It's one step away from total noise and
chaos, terrible and electric in the most epic way possible.

At my exit, I notice a new billboard. There's a responsible-looking woman, blandly attractive in an advertising sort of way, holding up a phone receiver with a look of professional concern on her face.

DEPRESSED? SUICIDAL? ADDICTED? THERE'S HELP. THERE'S HOPE. CALL 1-800-TALK-NOW.

I'm speeding along, singing the chorus, scowling and jabbing my finger at the responsible billboard woman when I realize that if I decipher "talk now," it's the number to the psych ward where I work. Nurses screen the calls and patch them through the crisis line to me. I am the woman on the billboard.

Help. Hope. *Hello?*

I can't be that woman. I'm neither responsible nor blandly attractive nor conscientious enough to show a professional level of concern. Who am I to get involved? It's not like I've got it together. Somebody probably needs to help me. And I hate drama. Maybe I should just forget any sort of career in mental health.

Yeah, God. Right, I pray, a little like Jonah at Jaffa's back gate. *If that's really the way I'm supposed to go in life, you're gonna have to send a better sign.*

I back up the track to the beginning, crank it louder, and shout along all the way home.

A week or so later I'm called to the ER at two in the morning to see a reedy Los Angelite with jet-black hair, his arms riddled with ink.

"Good luck getting anything out of this one," the doctor says before I push through the door to the patient's room.

Jet Black Angelite and I talk for a while. I try at least. He's skittish and shy, shaky from the meth, a long, long way from home. Then I notice a tattooed logo near his left wrist. "138," I say, pointing to the skull.

He turns and makes eye contact for the first time. "You *know* that song?" he asks.

"Is it time to be an android?" I reply, quoting the verse. "And not a man?"

"I tried so hard not to feel," he says, shaking his head. "But I just can't."

The room is quiet; Jet Black lays back, staring through the window at the parking lot lights. "I was sitting on the end of my bed with the razor in my hand, trying to get up the nerve to finish, and I prayed. And let me tell you something, I am not the kind of person who prays. I hadn't said any kind of prayer in a long, long time. But I prayed and said, *If there's any sort of God out there, then help me, please.*"

"So what happened?"

"You're gonna think I'm crazy, man."

"I'm the midnight psychiatric crisis guy. Try me."

"I had my iPod on shuffle and that song came on. I heard it and remembered back, remembered the way it made me feel so strong, like I could rise up over anything." He stretches his arm out and shows me a short row of slices stitched up down the side. "I had already made a bunch of practice cuts but I wrapped my arm in a towel and ran outside and there was a cab two streets over sitting at the curb. Man, there's no cabs in this town. You know how many cabs are in this town?"

"Two or three, maybe?"

"Maybe," he says. "So I ran over knowing any cab driver's

gonna see the blood and drive off with the doors locked. But when I got close this guy stepped out. He wasn't American, but I swear he looked just like those pictures of Jesus you see. Skinny, sort of long hair, beard—but it wasn't any of that, man. It was his eyes. And he put me in the cab and drove me here. I had two fives in my pocket and I tried to give them to him but he said, 'No, brother. Just you get help.'"

There's a long pause while his vital signs pulse across the screen. "And then this," Jet says. "I can't believe you know that song."

I sit silent, not really knowing what to say. When you work in ERs and psych wards you realize that pretty much every desperate person prays and God doesn't always come through. Not in obvious ways at least. A lot of times you wonder if sometimes he misses or avoids the call, or if that's just the way the world is supposed to be. When you get into the grit and dirt of things, life can be pretty hard to figure out. But if there's some small spark, you grab on to it. And that spark seems to be that in the dark, desperate places, we are all pretty much the same.

"Kinda strange the way things work, ain't it?"

"Yeah," he says. "It really is."

In the space of the doorframe we see an old man inching his way down the hall by gripping the rail. From the other direction, the nurse pushes a wheelchair; a bald woman with sunken eyes is slumped against the side. When they pass, the old man reaches out and for one brief second they touch hands.

"You know what else I prayed for, Jamie?" Jet Black says.

"What's that?"

He lifts a finger slowly and says, "Just one sign."

IT'S NEARLY DAWN BY THE TIME I GET BACK HOME, AND TO tell you the truth, I still feel unsure about a lot of things. Things like where I belong and what I'm supposed to be doing with my life, how to find the balance between responsibility and faith, how much is up to God and how much is on me, the strange ways he speaks and how to hear his voice above the noise.

Would God show up in the trashed-out apartment of a tattooed drug addict? Would he intervene through some punk rock anthem of agitation and youth? Would he send an Arab cab driver like an angel to intercede? Would he send somebody like me? I guess that depends on what kind of God you believe in.

There's a secret door in the wall behind the hedge, then another, then a spiral set of stairs to my room. A blanket thrown over the banister blocks out the morning sun. I've got the sounds of a thunderstorm playing on endless loop and a purple string of lights set like stars above my bed so I can watch them twinkle before I fall asleep. Brother Jet's in rehab. Checked him in myself. We shook hands on the patio before I headed home.

"If there's ever anything I can do for you," he said.

"Just one thing," I told him. "Say one of those prayers for me too, okay?"

"All right," Jet said, smiling. "I'll say one tonight."

I turned to go but he held tight to my hand. "You gotta keep doing this crazy midnight thing, man," he said. "There's places only a person like you can go."

"Ah, man, I don't know," I replied, working free from his grip. "Maybe so." Then I walked away, got in my truck, and drove home.

The stars are fading as the storm rolls in. Sometimes I feel like God leaves me hanging. But other times, it's like he answers on the very first ring.

TWENTY-ONE

BAD JAMIE AND THE OLD RUGGED CROSS

*"Remember those in prison, as if
you were there yourself."*

–HEBREWS 13:3 NLT

SOME COLLEGE BUDDIES AND I GO TO THE DISCOUNT movie theater. The movie is awful so we act like fools. There's a food fight, a stupid ruckus, blowing off steam. It's not so funny when the police arrive and take us to the city jail.

This isn't good, I think as the jailer walks me down the hall.

He places me in a short-timer side cell with five other guys. A squat, stocky man in a work shirt with *Romero* stiched on the pocket steps right up to me.

"Hey, Rock and Roll," he says. "Wha-choo in for, eh?"

For some reason I hang my head, drag my toe across the floor and say in the sad voice of Eeyore, "I shot some Mexicans."

He leans in closer and narrows his eyes. I crouch down and stare back. The cell gets very quiet.

Diego cracks up laughing, hugs me, and turns to the other guys. "This guy, we go to the same church sometimes!"

"What are you doing here?" I ask him.

"My old lady, like a fool I gave her the child support in cash. Then she claimed I didn't pay her. I had a few beers and . . ." Diego waves his hands in the air. "It's nothing, we work it out."

The other men gather round and introduce themselves. DUIs. Battery. Writing hot checks. Failure to yield.

"Failure to yield?"

"Lost the ticket and didn't pay the fine," No Yield Guy says. "What about you?"

"Riot at the dollar movie."

No Yield whistles as if he's impressed, as if I'd knocked off a jewelry store. "You really do it?" he asks.

"Naw, that was Bad Jamie," I tell him. "You know, that other me that does all those stupid things?"

"Yeah, I got one of those," No Yield says. "That guy is a total idiot."

A snowy old TV sits on a milk crate. "Hey," Diego says. "We can't catch nothin' but the Big Bird channel and *Nova* is on. We're about to get a game up if you want to play."

"Sure. What you got? Dominoes? Spades?"

Diego reaches under his bunk and pulls out a long box. "You know how to play *Clue*?"

"Are you kidding? I love *Clue*."

In the side cell of the city jail, board games with a church brother and a few new friends. We roll the dice and tell our stories, about sin and redemption and grace and regret. About that Bad Me that does all those stupid things. *Nova* drones softly in the background, the rings of Saturn covered in static and snow.

About the time I'm suspecting Colonel Mustard in the kitchen with the candlestick, a friend and her fiancé bail me out.

"Aw man, you gotta go already?" No Yield says, "You just got here."

Diego grabs my hand through the bars as I leave. "Hey, Jamie," he says. "Don't let this get you down, friend. You're a good dude. We all capable of the worst sometimes."

"I know, brother. Thanks."

The following Wednesday, I return to the jail's church service with my guitar and an antenna for the inmates' TV. Most of the guys are gone, but No Yield remains. When I ask him why, he just holds up his hands.

I'm in the corner getting tuned when a stooped old prisoner with a cane hands me a scrap of paper with the words *Old Rugged Cross* scratched in pencil, the letters shaky and big.

"If you know it," he says, his voice barely above a whisper.

"I know it," I tell him.

While I sing about that dark emblem he rests his forehead on the end of his cane, closes his eyes, and drifts far away.

After service, as he shuffles back to his cell, I slip him my last ten-dollar bill.

"God bless you," he says.

"He does," I reply.

I CHANGED MY MAJOR FIVE TIMES, FINALLY GRADUATED with a degree in psychology, and got a free ride to grad school because I used to skate with Dean Gage's daughter. The university pays me to go to class in the mornings and do primate studies at the zoo in the afternoons. When you're bottle-feeding baby goats on Lemur Island, God feels very close and all is right with the world. People? People are crazy. Behavioral psych suited me fine, until they told me I'd have to get my PhD to really do anything in the business. So I switched over to the master's in counseling psychology. I'd like to tell you my intentions were noble—to bring help and healing to a hurting world—but truth is, I changed mostly because the counseling degree requires no thesis.

It's late Thursday morning in Dr. Cryer's therapeutic methods class. The average counseling student is at least twice my age, divorced, weepy, struggling with sobriety, and deeply involved in dysfunctional relationships. Holiday sweaters and macramé necklaces. Flowbee haircuts and *Cat Fancy* magazine. Sitting near the back, I look like a third-rate Vegas magician or a clichéd Christ in a tourist trap's passion play.

Today, Cryer tells us that since the Bible—the bestselling and most influential book of all time—calls Jesus the wonderful counselor, perhaps we should take a look at the way he ran his practice.

Cryer says if we study the Jesus method, we'll learn that a wonderful counselor would listen and not judge, be patient and humble, and be able to explain things in regular, ordinary ways. A wonderful counselor would tell stories that help you come around to the truth on your own. You couldn't be all pushy and be called a wonderful counselor. You would have to be approachable and down-to-earth. Not uptight or churchy or desperate to fix things. Mostly, you'd have to be willing to go where the people need you, but balance yourself by stealing off alone for long retreats as well.

I ask Cryer, a deacon at his Southern Baptist church, if a

modern-day Jesus might take people out to smoke. Because that seems to be my key role in the helping industry thus far.

"Probably," says Cryer. "Because Jesus knows people at the end of their rope often smoke."

"How about all the cursing?" I ask. The other students turn and look back, as if one lever were attached to all of their heads. They're not used to me talking in class. Usually I slump down and draw on my notebook or nod off like a junkie. I am, however, the only person in the program with any real experience working in mental health.

Cryer walks from the board and sits at the corner of his desk. "Well, desperate people use desperate words. We learned in 101 you can't judge by the outer appearance. It's the counselor's job to dig deeper and find out the heart of things. And the only way to do that is be still and listen."

"Besides," adds Cryer, "if cigarette smoke and curse words bothered Jesus I don't think he would have picked a bunch of fishermen to work with."

Chuckling rumbles through the class. He juggles the chalk and walks back to the board. "You work at the psych ward last night, Mr. Blaine?" he asks, scribbling a quote from Nietzsche.

"Yes sir."

"Did you calm down any cussing people? Take anybody out to smoke?"

"Every night."

"Hang in there," Cryer says. "You just might make it yet."

TWENTY-TWO

PICK WONDER

"Creativity is the residue of time wasted."

–EINSTEIN

I PULLED A DOUBLE ON PSYCH LAST NIGHT–4:00 P.M. TO
7:00 a.m.—and it was one round after another of Thorazine
takedowns, rehab cuss fights, and all-out schizophrenic don-
nybrooks. Right as dawn broke and I was about to clock out,
a retired math teacher strung his belt to a sprinkler head and
jumped. I cut him down, did CPR, drove home, ate a giant bowl
of Cocoa Pebbles, and slept till the stars were out.

It's 11:30 now on a Tuesday night and the streets are wet
from an early evening rain. My mind is still spinning, so I ride
my bike to the Quik Stop, get three bucks in quarters, and head
back by the ICEE machine to play *Black Knight* pinball. I can
go thirty minutes or so on just fifty cents. I plug in my money;
with a screech the bumpers blaze and the Black Knight cackles.
Everything is neon and chrome.

When I was a kid, pinball was a hideout, a way to calm my mind. So here I am tonight at one of a few machines left around town. There are worse places I could be, worse things I could be doing. Better pinball than Xanax and wine.

While I wait for the ball, I catch my reflection in the window, just beneath the Pick 3 lottery and Malt Liquor Bull signs. My friends are buying homes and having babies, making their way up the ladder of life. I'm riding my Huffy to the Quik Stop to play pinball all night. At the moment, I can't decide whether I'm on top of the world or the bottom. I point to the figure in the glass.

There you are.

I wonder what Jesus was like in his twenties. Was he quiet and to himself? Easygoing? What did he do for fun? I wish there were a book in the Bible about Jesus at twenty-five, because I'd sure like to know. Wonder if Jesus would hang out with me. All my life I've heard that Jesus loves me—but would he like me? *Would I like Jesus?* We all wonder sometimes, don't we?

Would a twentysomething Jesus be here right now, his dirt bike leaning on the wall next to mine after a long day at the carpenter's shop, smiling that easy Jesus smile as we slap hands back by the ICEE machine? Would he lay fifty cents on the rail and laugh like he might not let me beat him so easily this time? Is it blasphemous to think about Jesus that way? Is too much scattered wonder sacrilegious?

Dear God, I hope not. 'Cause if it is, I'm doomed.

A Gulf Coast Power and Light truck roars by, spraying puddle water up over the lines. Orange hazards flash against the trees, then all is calm again. Time passes slower late at night. You can stand and stare out the window long as you like, just thinking, letting your mind run free.

If I were God coming to earth I would have arrived seven thousand feet tall with fiery eyes and lightning in my hair. Accompanied by a billion-member marching band and Day-Glo angels waving sparklers the size of the Sears Tower. To come down as a baby, a fugitive, a carpenter, a rebel, a criminal—a nobody? You have to admit, that's a strange twist. So I don't believe Jesus was some supercharismatic evangelist, or the world's greatest CEO, or an ultimate life coach, or anything extraordinary like that. I think God came down to earth as a regular guy with workman's hands and sawdust in his shoes. That's what makes the story so good.

But what if those uptight religious people are right? Because their Jesus is standing outside, staring at me, and sadly shaking his head. And if that's how Jesus really is, I don't know what to do. Really, I don't. I worry about that sometimes.

But you know, there's this principle Jesus taught once he was out of the carpenter shop and into his ministry. He said that between worry and wonder, pick wonder every time.

Also, I'm pretty sure he told the people something like this:

Hey, don't worry too much about tomorrow. Whatever happens, I'm with you. And even if this life is one long ramble, stumbling in circles and trying to find the doors, I've still got a surprise for you at the end. There is no end. So don't take it all too seriously. Just take it as it comes. Even if you wreck everything and end up a thousand miles lost out in the dark—I'll come find you. I'll meet you right where you are and help you back toward home.

So let others know that's who I am. Because everybody's

struggling down here. Let's be patient and good to each other. We're all in this thing together, my friend.

That's the Jesus I believe in. That's the message that gives me hope. But truth is, I just don't know. It's only what I hope. Someday when I finally sit down with God on the levees of heaven we will have a long, long talk about this thing called life.

"Storm's moving back in," Eazy Stevie, the Quik Stop cashier, calls over. "You can park your bike in the back room if you want."

Rain on asphalt. Taillights down a long, dark street. The silver ball waits as the Black Knight taunts me into the game. A truck marked JC Brothers Towing pulls up, and there's a sticker back by the gas cap that says "Live Free or Die." Maybe the signs are everywhere, if you just slow down and open your eyes.

Stevie keeps a radio on the end of the back shelf. "Midnight showers, drive safe, and make it a . . . 'Slow Ride'!" the DJ croaks. Four on the floor, the bass drum thumps, Lonesome Dave's guitar wails like a siren in the night.

"All right," Stevie whispers as she turns it up.

I pull back the plunger and fire.

TWENTY-THREE

TREASURES IN THE DARK

"Push out into deep water."

−JESUS, LUKE 5:4 ISV

IT'S JUST AFTER MEDS, AND I'VE TAKEN MY PATIENTS OUT for the last smoke of the night. Everybody's passing around the pack of community cigarettes, lighting them end to end, people at the end of their ropes talking about love and sex and work and God and trying to make it through one day at a time.

The smoke break often slips into a little reprobate Bible study before bed. Nothing fancy or planned. Just fifteen cigarettes glowing in the dark, a flashlight, and motel Bible. Old drunks and outlaws, loose women, outcasts, losers, dope fiends, failed suicides, and schizophrenics reading about the peace that passes understanding, grace that trumps all sin, and a love and forgiveness that knows no end.

"Listen to this," the lady they call Crazy Mary says. "He leads me beside still waters and restores my soul."

"Still waters," Lonnie, a jilted pillhead, echoes back. "Sure could use some of that."

Everyone nods, letting the notion sink in. Late nights at the psych ward can be pretty peaceful sometimes. No rush. No hurry. Nowhere to go but up from here.

There's a black gentleman, a retired former deacon, given to whiskey after his wife died. He's got a grey afro and scraggly beard and has become something of a leader to the group, so the other patients nicknamed him Moses. He slips a pair of glasses from the pocket of his red plaid shirt and reads a passage from the book of Job about darkness and the whirlwind, and everybody stares at the ground, shaking their heads.

"Lotta stuff in there I can't understand," Lonnie says.

"Me neither," Moses replies. "But it's them parts I do that bother me most."

"I hear you," says Lonnie.

Moses leans across the circle and hands the Bible to Keith.

Keith's hair sticks up, he's got a bad stutter, and his mouth hangs open most all the time. He wears charity glasses from the Lion's Club—a thick, old, pewter-framed pair that sits crooked on his head, and he shuffles from the psychotropic meds. He's mentally challenged, actively psychotic, and has been in and out of prison and group homes all of his life. Keith has been on acute ward lockdown for a month now, and I could get in trouble just for bringing him out. But I promised Keith if he didn't cuss anybody or throw anything all evening, I would take him out to smoke with the patients from the other side. He kept his end of the deal and I'm keeping mine.

"Mr. Keith," Moses says. "It's your turn."

"I-I only, uh . . . I only know one," Keith says, hands shaking and head down.

"That's okay," says Moses. "Just read the one you know."

Keith thumbs through the Bible for the longest time. Then he puts his face close to the page and slowly begins to read. "For G-God," he says. "So loved . . . th-the world. That he gave . . . he gave his . . . gave his o-only . . ."

"It's all right, baby," Crazy Mary says. "Take your time."

He draws a deep breath and in a soft, clear voice says, "His only son. That whoever b-believes in him . . . would have life."

Keith closes the Bible and turns off the light. And in the dark, silent spaces, the Spirit rushes in.

I wish I could gather my church and show them this moment. There are lessons here we all need. Every day it seems the patients are teaching me to look for the good, to not believe everything I think, that often the best prayer is simply, *Help me, please.* They show me that God is so close to the lost and broken—closer in many ways than the religious can ever be. Jesus said that first, you know.

"Be careful," Jesus taught. "Those people you call lost are actually closer to the kingdom than you."

Jesus still speaks and walks among us through those we call the least, through old drunks and outcasts and the terminally depressed. There is a truth found only at rock bottom and the end of the rope—treasures in the dark, hidden riches in the secret place.

If I ever need to see mercy and grace in action all I have to do is bring a really sick patient over from PICU. If I take someone over who is an absolute wreck, the addicts and depressed patients will step up and show so much compassion and love. It's a reminder that in our finest moments we really do take care of each other down here. When we drop our agendas and realize that as long as we are obsessing over self we will continue to die inside. But when we meet each other in that honest place, past labels and divisions and petty disputes, when we pick each other up and pretend to be nothing other than exactly who we are, the truly supernatural can occur. I don't want to knock church, but something's missing. It's not the same. Maybe we're not desperate enough. Maybe we're too busy putting on the show. Man, I don't know.

A few months back I pulled some strings, risked a lot of trouble, and came in on my day off to take a van load of psych-ward patients to church. We weren't treated like lepers. But we weren't exactly welcomed either. I probably shouldn't tell that story. But it's true. In fact, it's more than true. I didn't try just once; I tried three times at three different churches. And the results were the same. I don't know what to do with that. I'm not mad at anybody, and I don't want to criticize, but it confuses me. It really breaks my heart.

I think we made the church people uncomfortable. Maybe they didn't know what to say. Maybe for some, it hit too close to home—too much of a reminder that if it weren't for grace, that could be them. Truth is, it was awkward for everybody, and I wished I hadn't done it. I wished we had just stayed at the psych ward and had our own kind of church.

In many ways this psych-ward courtyard is the lowest place there is. I've heard patients say it's worse than jail even, to be locked up not because you broke the law but because you lost your mind. Because you can't stay sober. Because you just can't hold life together anymore.

And yet . . .

There is a hope here so raw and so real that there is no doubt that God is in this place.

I love the shiny, happy Jesus from church, but there is another side—that dark-eyed Lord of Glory with dirt beneath his nails. The troublemaking Son of God who shows up when drunks march in courtyards and cry that life is unfair. The Christ who is there when schizophrenics throw chairs and just want to go home. The Light of the World who loves people in the lowest place. The King of Peace who turns over tables and makes water into wine. The Great High Priest whose good news went something like this:

No matter who you are,
where you are,
or how far gone,
there is always a way back home.

I'm about to call it a night when Keith shuffles over and hands the Bible to me. "H-here, Jamie," he says. "You didn't g-get a turn."

I fumble with the flashlight, flipping through pages. There's just one verse I want to read, a line I once heard a crying preacher recite at the funeral of a prodigal who never could make it toward home. It takes awhile but finally I find my place.

"Matthew fifteen," I read. "And Jesus healed them all."

The circle is quiet as I pass the Bible back. Moses stands and leads us to the door.

"E-everybody?" asks Keith, as we wait.

I turn the key; the electro-locks fire and we pass through,

shading our eyes from the bright lights of the hall. Lonnie lays his hand on Keith's shoulder before I walk him away. "Hey, brother," he says. "We'll see you tomorrow, right?"

"S-sure," says Keith. "All right."

IT'S SUNDAY EVENING, NEARLY TWO YEARS AFTER I STARTED working at the psych ward. Pastor Reddy catches me in the church foyer after service and calls me over. With his curly wisp of hair and ear-to-ear smile, he reminds me of a middle-aged Charlie Brown. "How's the mental health mission field going?" he asks.

I try to find a way to sum it up, to compose the right words to where the pastor can understand. "Remember when you said God could use me to change those people?" I ask him. "To teach them about the Lord?"

"Yuh," he says. "How goes it?"

"Pastor, I think they're teaching me about Jesus," I tell him. "I think God's using those people to change me."

Reddy looks at me kind of sideways a minute before he speaks. "Well," he says, "I guess we help change and teach each other. Can I pray for you?"

"Yeah, sure," I say, closing my eyes.

He places his hand on the back of my neck and bows his head. "Father," he says. "Watch out for your boy here. Guide him with wisdom and protection and help him walk in kindness and bring light and life and goodness wherever he goes. We ask these things, in your name, amen."

"Amen," I agree. There's a silence after genuine prayer, like Genesis again, like liquid peace poured over your soul. "So you, uh, think I oughta stick with it?"

"Son," he says. "We got too many preachers that know how to talk; not nearly enough that know how to listen."

"I don't know if I'm cut out for that preacher part."

"Ministry," Pastor Reddy says, pointing through the front glass to the Git-R-Dunn car wash and the Laundromat just past the liquor store, "is out there."

"Yes sir," I tell him. "I'll try."

"Just do your best," he says, giving me a quick hug before walking away.

"Hey Pastor," I call. "Is it wrong to ask for a sign or somethin'?"

"I got faith in you, brother," he calls back. "You'll find your way."

TWENTY-FOUR

OF POMP AND CIRCUMSTANCES

"A good traveler has no fixed plans
and is not intent on arriving."

–LAO LAOZI

IT'S MY LAST SEMESTER AND DR. CRYER ASSIGNS A FINAL report based on Albert Camus' *The Stranger*. From there, I read Karl Barth and Franz Kafka, Bonhoeffer and Tillich and Søren Kierkegaard, Viktor Frankl and crazy old Freddie Nietzsche, Christ and Ecclesiastes from a different point of view.

I ponder existential theories, confusion, and futility in what often seems like a meaningless world. The paradox of God and man, beauty and chaos, freedom and loss, the significance of questioning everything and the liberty of embracing the absurd. Misfit Jesus and the irony of a God who shrouds himself in darkness and takes glory in concealing things.

I start studying the whole Bible, not just the parts that are evangelically approved. Blood to the bridles of horses and rebel angels having sex with the daughters of men. Stuttering, angry Moses, denied the promised land; lustful, murdering David, a man after God's own heart; Solomon's wisdom neutered by concubines; Ezekiel's wheel of fire in the sky; kamikaze Samson and his suicide mission from on high; the prophet Hosea ordered to marry a whore; the only Son of God who brawled in church and vanished for days at a time, whose own family came to take him away because they were certain he had lost his mind.

One night, I'm going through *Twilight of the Idols,* giving Nietzsche an amen, then nearly get choked up watching Mr. T preach on TBN. I write till the sun rises, turn in a pile of rambling but passionate pages, and score my first 100 A+. At the top of my paper, Cryer writes in red, "Good work, Mr. Blaine. Maybe you've finally found your niche."

IT'S A LATE-MAY SATURDAY AFTERNOON AND I'M SITTING second row at graduation, together with all the other students getting their master's. Several of the students around me are crying, and the girl to my right grips a picture of two kids in her locket and keeps whispering, "Thank you, Jesus; thank you, Lord."

The marching band bleats out the theme from *Cats* while we all sweat and fan ourselves with the programs. Some bald joker who owns a pizza joint gives a commencement speech that smells like a pitch for a pyramid scheme. I plod across the stage when they call my name. Dean Gage hands me a diploma, winks, and says, "You made it."

The diploma is fake—a blank page with a tiny, rolled-up

note inside saying the real one should arrive by mail in the next two to six weeks. The graduation is over; no one throws their hat. I stash my diploma in the glove box and drive straight from campus to work at the rink.

On the way over I think about how it all seems a little empty, the fake ceremony, fake diploma, faking my way through. It feels like poor metaphor. I need a better metaphor—a ceremony with more weight. So I duck through the Skate City back door and change straight out of cap and gown into the Roller Rabbit costume. Mr. Ric walks by while I'm wrestling on the pants.

"Aren't you supposed to be graduating?" Mr. Ric asks, arching his left brow.

"Just did," I tell him. "Wanna see my diploma?"

"I bet we're the only rink in the world whose DJ's got a master's degree," he laughs. "So what are you gonna do now?"

Furry pants and cottontail fixed, I slip on the oversized bunny head and tweak my ears. "The hokey pokey," I reply.

Calling skaters to a circle in the center of the floor, I roll out to meet them as the bouncy old disco version begins to play. There's smoke and lights and loud, loud music. Happy children make a joyful noise. *Nietzsche and Mr. T., Solomon, Job, and Jesus . . . This one's for you.*

"Ladies and gentlemen," Ric announces on the mic. "Give it up for Dr. Roller Rabbit!" I spin on my skates and do a little hustle side to side. There's a flash as Nikki rolls by to snap a few shots. The children cheer; they laugh and sing; they hug me and tug at my tail.

Maybe this really is what it's all about.

It's late by the time I leave. My ears are ringing from all the noise, and I am exhausted in the best possible way. Nikki gave me a printout of one of the pictures she took, a blurry shot of Roller Rabbit, surrounded by happy kids. Long hair hangs from the bottom of the bunny head, and if you look hard enough you can see my face through the mesh in Roller Rabbit's mouth, eyes laughing, smile wide. As I'm backing out to leave, Mr. Ric taps my glass and motions the window down.

"Seriously," he says. "Now that you've graduated, what are you going to do?"

"I don't have the first clue."

"Sure could use a good manager," he says, pressing a set of keys into my hand. "Maybe just for a while, until something better comes along."

"Something else might come along someday," I tell him, glancing at the picture. "But never anything better."

"All right, then," Mr. Ric says. "We've got a private party for Chelsea tomorrow afternoon. See you then."

I prop the photo against my speedometer, holding the keys to the rink, sliding my fingers along the teeth. I'm probably the only guy in the history of the world who just got a master's degree and took an assistant manager position at a roller rink. I was kind of worried that when I graduated things would change, that maybe I would have to leave the rink. That might happen someday. But not today. Not for a long time. As ceremonies go, that's pretty fine.

It's nearly summer now but still cool enough to ride at night with the windows down. Some students celebrated graduation by buying new cars or first houses, getting married and settling down. I've got seven bucks and some change in my pocket. But I guess I really should do something to commemorate the occasion, so I pull into the Quik Stop to get a peach ICEE for the ride. There's a crusty old guy in a blood-donor tee sitting on the curb down by the Dumpster at the side of the store. He's got a beagle pup cradled in his arms and a tall paper sack sitting by his tennis shoe. We exchange nods as I slip through the Quik Stop door. A small ICEE is eighty-nine cents, but you can get the super-size for a dollar forty-nine in a collectable cup with Batman on the side. I look back and forth trying to make up my mind, knowing what I need to do. I get the small, taking one long sip at the machine and filling it back up before I snap on the lid. Pay the cashier, head out the door, down to the curb. Hand the change to the crusty old man.

"Here you go, brother."

He folds the money into his pocket, smiling once it's tucked away. "What if I take your money and buy somethin' bad?"

"You can buy whatever you want," I tell him. "I gave it to you. It's your money now."

He reaches over, opens the tall sack, and pulls out an empty can of Shep dog food, the lid jagged, hacked open with a knife. "We run out this afternoon," he says. "Glad you come by."

"What's your dog's name?"

"Lady," he says, ruffling her ears. "You wanna hold her?"

"Yes sir," I tell him. "Yeah, I do."

He passes Lady into my arms. At first she trembles, then she presses her cold nose against my neck and licks the side of my face.

"She smells that candy," Crusty says. "Why you smell like cotton candy?"

God in heaven works in mysterious ways, in strange places and situations that often don't make one bit of sense. But when he arrives, you know. Eleven-thirty at night, sitting on the Quik

Stop curb, summer breeze drifting, and for just one moment the world makes sense, even if only for a little while.

"Hey, I graduated today," I tell old Crusty. "Got myself a master's degree."

"Congratulations," Crusty says. "That's nice. That's real, real fine."

PART THREE

SCARS, STARS, AND JESUS IN THE DARK

"It has always been the prerogative of children and half-wits to point out that the emperor has no clothes. But the half-wit remains a half-wit, and the emperor remains an emperor."

—NEIL GAIMAN

*"Then the L*ORD *answered Job from the whirlwind."*

—JOB 38:1 NLT

TWENTY-FIVE

LIKE CHAINSAW JUGGLING OR WRESTLING BEARS

"I started to realize that there was a great hunger and
thirst for regular, cynical, ragbag people to talk about
God and goodness and virtue in a tone that didn't
frighten and upset you, or make you feel that you
were doing even more poorly than you'd thought."

–ANNE LAMOTT

THE CHRISTIAN COUNSELING CENTER SITS IN THE SHADOW
of the sanctuary of one of the largest churches in America. It's
in a small, Southern town, Super Walmart and Friday-night
football, stickers on pickup trucks proclaiming the gospel of the
fair-haired, Southern Jesus. Not the most likely place for church-
based psychotherapy. Many here are far more willing to discuss
the problems of others before their own, but the former pastor, a
sweet, lanky, saint of a guy, had the foresight to start a ministry
devoted just to listening.

They chose my old psych ward comrade Garrett Thomas to get the ball rolling, giving him a run-down building off the main campus, filled with mismatched cans of pastel paint, stacks of old magazines, and some secondhand furniture. After I got my master's, he graciously offered me a job. It's only part-time so I'll still have to hustle, managing the rink and pulling crisis call for the psych ward here and there.

But that's all right. I'm not real sure about working for the church anyway; I've been limited to sitting in the balcony or far back, just watching. There's security in community and becoming part of a movement; and though a lot of people bash big ministries, I've seen a lot of good come from this sort of organization. I think maybe I can help some people, and even straighten myself up along the way.

I am going to try to participate and go to staff meetings and wear semidecent clothes so I don't look like a ticket scalper at a Tampa Bay Van Halen concert. I'll try to be a team player and on board with the church's mission statement to offer "supportive, empathetic listening in a caring atmosphere of hope, healing, and restoration," even though there's something about estrogen-heavy church slogans that make me want to run away and become a fire-breathing freak in a sideshow circus.

I've never done any actual sit-down counseling, but I figure I can fake it till I make it. Maybe they'll send me people struggling with the theological/philosophical meaning of life, and why the Bible seems so mean and crazy sometimes with the whole Job and Moses thing—with six-winged creatures covered with eyes and locust armies and wild women driving tent stakes through the temples of men.

I black out my office windows and shut down the lights

except for a lone, amber lamp on a corner desk. I've got a sea-green Naugahyde lounger and an old couch so worn-out and low your feet barely touch the floor once you sink into its folds. White noise to block out the world, Eno for ambience sometimes. And when the clients are gone and the whole therapeutic thing is too weird and melodramatic to take, I blast a little Motörhead to balance things out.

For a while I fear being exposed, that people will discover that even though I work at the church, I'm still pretty messed up and unsure about a lot of spiritual things. Soon enough I figure out I'm not the only one faking it. Not by far. I learn that what people claim corporately and believe privately are two very different things. I discover that when you get hurting people in a dark room, hurting enough to be honest, they will tell you things that make you realize we are all struggling and stumbling and wrestling with God and wondering what's really going on down here.

I'm shaky but thankful, praying maybe I can finally find my place within the church and work thing. I realize God doesn't always call people to a conventional way. Some are called to the fringe, to the outsider and the misfit, to dark rooms, the balcony, and the far-back pew. My plan is to lay low, stick to the places I know, and try to stay out of trouble.

WHEN I TELL PEOPLE I WORK AT A CHURCH COUNSELING center, they often reply with something like, "What kind of problems do church people have?"

There's a cute girl with freckles—a pretty good kid who sings Sunday mornings, makes good grades when she wants to, and just about every weekend sneaks out of her window to meet with the neighborhood boys. And lately, the neighborhood girls.

"She grew up in church," the mother cries. "We did everything we could."

Last week there were beautiful, bright children who cut their skin in secret places. Yesterday it was a Sunday school teacher who drinks herself to sleep. At two o'clock it was a single dad with cancer trying to raise his daughter alone, and after that a starving young bride going bald from anxiety and eating disorders. On tomorrow's calendar, there's a pastor who preaches peace but says he's never known any, and a fifty-five-year-old man who just can't grow up.

Dead marriages and depressive fatigues. Ungovernable teens, phantom lusts, deviant compulsions, chemical addictions. Doubts, fears, anxiety in the night. Lost God. Suicide.

And this is what I do: listen a lot, talk a little, hear all sorts of crazy things. Try to steer and do damage control. I practice psychological magic and distraction. And when that doesn't work (which is often) I pray elaborate, eloquent prayers of great spiritual depth, like *helpGodhelpGodhelp*, and become quite certain there are easier ways to make a little money. Like chainsaw juggling or wrestling bears.

I encourage, prod, provoke when appropriate. I promote reality, balance, peace, and the understanding that peace must be seized and faith does not remove responsibility. I quote Axl Rose and Jesus, King Solomon and Hunter S. Thompson.

"You can't save nobody else," I remind them. "You can't even save yourself."

"Call on God," I urge, "but row away from the rocks."

And still, people grasp frantically for control and row back into the rocks again and again.

"Me too," I confess. I struggle with those same doubts and fears and anger and lust and longing for something I cannot quite explain. The same feeling that there's some unknown x in the algebra of God that I will never be able to figure out. That even with all the combined powers of theology, psychology, philosophy, and the good guidance of the evangelical church, I am still grasping frantically and steering toward the rocks, doomed to screw it all up and hit every pothole from here to heaven.

And if there is one thing I can tell people for certain—something that might be helpful—it is this: "Me too."

But sometimes it's almost like I feel called to preach. It's a bone-deep feeling, like the time between thirst in the desert and taking that first cold drink. I want to tell the people to burn all their flags and embrace the illogical. To speak truth, fight the power, and truly be like history's most infamous radical, that rebel Jesus Christ.

Not if I want to keep my job though.

TIME CRAWLS AND THE CLOCK TICKS LOUDLY. AN ATTRAC-tive, middle-aged mother of two sits before me. She has a sensible elegance, a warm smile, and her eyes are desperate but kind. She lives in a nice home, volunteers at the church, is active in the community, and has just revealed to me that most every night she dreams of ways to end her life. Guns and pills and suicide leaps. Car crashes and cocktails laced with bleach.

"I've even thought of going to Alaska and falling asleep in the snow," she says with a soft laugh that breaks my heart.

When I waved her in from the waiting room she was reading the latest book from a popular female evangelist. She stood and smiled, pausing to offer words of encouragement to the lady in the next chair down. In the office she spoke with pride about her children, their good grades and success in sports. She gave thanks for her husband's patience and praised him for being a good father and provider. In a whisper she said life was wearing her down and that no pill or prayer or program had given relief.

"Do you really believe all suicides go to hell?" she asks.

I don't know.

A fragile old man sits on my couch with his head in his hands, ragged fringes of gray poking between his fingers. He wears a worn suit jacket, long out of fashion, the sleeves too short.

"Now, she is gone," he says, the words measured and low. "No one to cut my hair. No more crossword puzzles together. No one to come home to. No more evening walks just talking and watching as the sun goes down."

He stares at his hands, twisting the gold band on his finger. "Every night, I would iron her skirts for work so she would have them the next morning." His eyes drift up into mine. "Been three months." His voice drops to a whisper. "I still iron every night." There is an ocean of grief between us, and my faith feels far too weak to bridge the gap.

"Thirty-seven years ago, we built our house. Behind every panel of sheetrock, on every brick and beam, we drew hearts in chalk. *G loves L. L loves G.* Now she's gone. And gone just hurts like hell."

It's like watching a scene from some sad, awful movie, only I realize he is here with me and it is all too real.

"What am I supposed to do now?" he asks. "Can you please tell me how am I supposed to move on?"

I don't know.

I don't know why life can be so beautiful and difficult almost in the same breath. It is the only honest thing I can say, and I hate it. I hate not knowing, I hate the way it makes me feel so helpless. You would think after all the school and study, after the seminars and sermons, I would have something figured out. You know what I figured out? You know what I know? Just how much I do not know.

"Realizing that you don't know," an old preacher once told me, "is where true wisdom begins."

Last appointment of the day. A big bouncy woman with a bright-red bob fidgets on the edge of my couch.

"I wouldn't want this gettin' around the church," she says, her eyes giddy, the tone of her voice saucy and sweet, like a late-night, lonely-hearts chat line. "So, this *is* confidential—right?"

Believe it or not, some come to gossip under the guise of counsel. Hey, my job is to listen, not judge. I settle back and give her a knowing smile.

"Oh yes," I whisper in the dark.

TWENTY-SIX

SUNSHINE SOMEDAY, MAYBE

"Secret things belong to the Lord."

—DEUTERONOMY 29:29 ESV

THERE'S A GIRL AT CHURCH NAMED KATY WHO SHOWS UP late and leaves early, sitting in the balcony back pew. She's a dancer, so I've heard. Not ballet.

"Somebody told me you're a counselor here," Katy says, catching me on the stairs, "and you work at the mental hospital, right?"

"I'm also the DJ at the skating rink."

"Yeah," she says, "I heard that too."

"What can I do for you?"

"I've got a friend in trouble," Katy tells me.

"What kind of trouble?"

"Trouble like bad," she says, voice cracking. "You think maybe you could talk to her? Please?"

"Yeah, sure," I reply. "Just tell me when and where."

It's midnight and I'm knocking on the back door of a seedy

club off Jefferson and Ninth. A big, bald bouncer who looks like a buff Uncle Fester ushers me in and goes to fetch Katy. Girls strut through the club, dressed in the typical stereotypes. Asian schoolgirl. Sassy cheerleader. Bad cop in hot pants, twirling her cuffs. A platinum blonde sashays by who could be a dead ringer for Britney Spears, if Britney broke her nose and drove a forklift for the lumber yard.

There's a *Black Rose* pinball machine near the back, so I plug in two quarters just as the DJ cues up "Gimme Three Steps" and welcomes Dixie to the stage. Before I can hit the flippers twice a girl grabs my arm and spins me around. She's dressed in a Western vest with chaps over tight satin pants, gold pigtails, and a ten-gallon hat.

"Hurry," Katy begs, cursing and jerking back her wig. "She just locked herself in the bathroom!"

She drags me through a mirrored panel hidden stage right, and we run down a low, dark hall with red dome lights toward a black door at the end. Katy pounds on it and yells for Sunshine. Big Fester arrives and puts his shoulder to the door. It collapses and we rush in. There's a girl scrunched in the corner, tears streaming down her face.

"Sunshine!" Katy shouts. "What did you *do?*"

Sunshine's lashed into a shiny black corset and tiger lilies are tattooed up the sides of both thighs. I pry open her fist and it is full of pills. Katy slaps her hand and they scatter across the floor. Sunshine's palm is stained yellow and pink.

"How many you take?" I ask, checking her pupils and pulse.

"Not enough," she slurs.

"Why?" I ask, and she shakes her head slowly from side to side.

There's one dim bulb over the bathroom sink and the walls are covered with sleazy graffiti, like a sex-obsessed Jackson Pollock with a Sharpie and Tourette's. Scrawled in a clear spot near the floor:

love is risk / love is pain / love never ever lets go

"Sunshine's been selling herself," Katy explains.

"What's that mean?"

"For drugs," says Katy. "I used to but I quit."

In the smallest, most broken voice Sunshine says, "I wanna quit too."

Big Fester scoops her up and we race out the back door. "I'm sorry, sorry," Sunshine cries. "I didn't want to hurt nobody else. Just myself."

"My car," yells Katy, throwing me the keys. "Take mine."

She leads us to a two-tone tan Cutlass Ciera and we wedge Sunshine between us in the front bench seat. When I buckle her in, she looks me over and asks, "Who's this guy?"

"Jamie works at my church," says Katy. "But he's cool."

Fester runs into the street and blocks traffic so we can leave. Just before we turn he sticks his head in the window and presses a ten and three ones into Sunshine's pill-stained hand. "Get better," he says. "Okay?"

Sunshine squeezes his fingers and forces a smile. "I'll try."

It's quiet in the car, driving up Seventh to Highway 39. Sunshine shifts in the curve and falls against me, a string of drool spilling down my shirt.

"She's not a bad person," Katy says, clicking the radio on low. "She's just made a lot of bad mistakes."

"Made a few myself," I confess.

"You think she'll be all right?"

"Tonight?"

Katy shakes her head, "After tonight."

"Don't know," I reply. "What do you think?"

"I think God forgives us," Katy says. "The hard part's living with yourself."

A slim silver pendant sways beneath the rearview mirror while Light Rock 106 plays a song about all the winding roads and blinding lights that lead us home. It fades and Lionel Richie begins to sing, saying he knows it sounds funny but he just can't stand the pain.

"What if we never really find a way to be all right?" I ask. "Then what?"

Katy reaches for the pendant, turning it so I can read. *God grant me the serenity.* She flips it to the other side. *To accept the things I cannot change.* The pendant swings again as she cracks the side window to smoke.

"I don't know, Jamie," she says, the ember glowing. "Guess that's why we sing 'Amazing Grace.'"

There is a fourth man in the fire, in silence and dark cars. In a beat-up Cutlass rolling toward the psych ward with two strippers in the front and a roller rink DJ-turned-psychotherapist at the wheel.

"Amen, sister. That's good," I tell her. "Maybe someday you could come work at the church too."

"Someday," says Katy, in a raspy whisper. "Maybe."

Sunshine's head is on my shoulder. She's snoring now. I turn down the hospital's long drive. Beyond the trees, a far light shines.

"Sunshine, wake up, baby," Katy says, pulling her face back straight and pushing the hair out of her eyes. "You're gonna make it. We're almost there."

TWENTY-SEVEN

BELIEVE THE BEST

*"You will do foolish things, but
do them with enthusiasm."*

–SIDONIE-GABRIELLE COLETTE

ON THURSDAYS I GO STRAIGHT FROM THE CHURCH COUN-
seling center to work at the rink. I like to get there early so I can
skate around the empty floor before we open. There's something
about rolling slow across a dimly lit floor.

The front door opens and my coworkers arrive, so I skate
up to meet them. "Whose birthday we got tonight?" I ask Jessie
while Jenny turns on the snack bar lights.

"No birthday tonight," she says. "Private party."

"Private?" I reply. "Who?"

Jessie points out to the parking lot. "Them."

Plastic girls everywhere, same perfect clothes, same perfect
hair, gaggled up and giggling, streaming toward the rink.

Jessie reads it from the calendar. "The Inter-Greek Spring
Fling Mixer."

"The what?" I ask.

"Sorority girls," Jessie answers. "Seventy-six of 'em."

"I'll get the door."

The girls pour in, smelling of sweet tanning lotion and the distinct stench of cheap Mexican food from Los Pollos Locos next door.

"Whooo, chicas!" I say, waving my hand in front of my face as a pack files by. "Burritos y margaritas?"

"You know it!" shout five blondes who look exactly the same.

They strap into skates and wobble to the floor. I kill the lights and call out over the mic, *"All the ladies in the house say?"*

Seventy-seven voices whoop it at once. *"Ho-oh!"*

While the intro to "Brick House" kicks in I hit ten spinning disco balls, both banks of strobe lights, and all the smoke machines at once. The sorority girls scream and throw their hands in the air. I am the only boy in a building filled with fun-time girls.

"This is the greatest job ever in the history of the world," I tell Jenny, a shy education major with a runway model's twiggy physique.

"I think a few of these girls might be tipsy," she says in a deadpan voice.

"These fine young ladies?" I say in their defense. "No way."

As "Brick House" fades I flash all the lights and segue straight into "Party Train." KDs, Phi Mus, and AOΠs singing and bumping behinds, dancing with hands to the sky.

The atmosphere plateaus when a dumpy green bus from the group home rattles up to the rink's front door. A tired woman leads in a cluster of ragamuffins, awkward children with dirty faces in tattered, mismatched clothes. They press in behind the woman, holding hands and grasping at the seam of her pants, staring out to the disco black lights and darling gaggles of roller-boogie sorority girls.

"It's a private party," we explain, in the kindest possible way. Jenny is handing the woman a consolation prize of free passes for family night when the sorority leader skates up with her second-in-command.

Both have ribbons in their hair that match their shorts and the T-shirts with their names embroidered on the front. *Abby. Emily.* They stand with hips cocked, staring at the woman and her raggedy clan. We are stuck in the middle, waiting for someone to speak.

"Are they staying?" Abby asks.

"It's your party," I tell her. "Up to you."

Emily leans down with her hands on her knees and looks the children over. A smile breaks over her face.

"Y'all like to skate?" she asks. The kids nod and squeal and squiggle with glee.

"Hush, now," the woman says to the children and they do. Quiet but giggly and ready to burst. "How much is it tonight?" she asks, riffling through her purse. "For a group?"

"We'll have to count and figure," Jenny says, shooting me a knowing look. "Just go ahead and let them start getting skates."

"Are you sure?" the woman says to Abby and Emily.

"We're sure," they reply. "Of course."

I stand to the side and fan out my hand, like Willy Wonka at the factory gates. "All right, kids," I say. "Are you ready?"

In a screaming frenzy, the children rush the counter. The sorority girls meet them there, unlacing shoes and helping with skates. They hold their hands and lead them around the floor.

It was happy before, but everything now is brighter and higher, the music louder, the mix of group-home kids and college girls, skating, helping, falling down, hooting and laughing and having a good time.

I autopilot the music and pocket the wireless mic. Jessie, Jenny, and I meet them on the floor for the Crazy Trio, a roller-rink game where you lock arms and skate in threes to the tune of "Green Onions." When the whistle blows, the trio turns and goes the opposite direction, "cracking the whip," as fast as you possibly can. From the pile of bodies, a new trio begins. I'm rolling backward between Jessie and Jenny, and it's quite the sight: thirty little urchins squealing with joy, grabbing grimy hands with sparkly sorority girls in pressed shorts and perfect ponytails.

"This is the greatest job ever," I shout as we fling each other round. "In the history. *Of the world.*"

"We know," Jessie says, just before she kicks my skates out from under me. "You told us already."

After we've fallen all over each other ten or twenty times, I end up in the middle of Abby and Emily. "Hey, just put those kids on our bill," Abby says, like it's no big deal.

"You don't have to do that," I tell her.

"We know," says Emily with a grin. "But it's more fun this way."

The funky organ of "Green Onions" grinds. The whistle blows again and again. We spin and crash and fall and laugh and laugh.

At the end of the night I send Jenny and Jessie on home. There's something strange and peaceful about a building that was so loud and full of life, dark and quiet now.

I flip the disco balls back to spinning and walk out to the floor. There are eight mirrored spheres in the center, from giant to small, and two more on each end.

If you lie flat in the middle of the floor it seems like some superspectacular solar system, with spotlight suns and sparkling planets, speckles of lights swarming the black like an ocean of stars. I lay on my back, staring, thinking about the world turning, reflecting light, billions of lives rising from the dust, everybody trying to find their place, trying to do the best they can before returning to dust again.

After a long time under the stars, I walk back to the front, flick the switch, and the rink fades until another day.

I HEAD HOME, PARK, FETCH MY BIKE, AND PEDAL SLOWLY down Sweet Olive Lane. I'm here nearly every night now. Lights in the trees down a long, dark road, the dusky shepherd loping beside me just before the curve. Weaving through the sprinklers, riding the levee to the riverbank below.

But tonight I take the last right before the dead-end sign and cut across Calla Lily Way to Bee Balm Avenue. Bee Balm runs parallel to Sweet Olive but continues on, catching the river's inlet beyond the bridge. The houses are newer but just as big, the streets so quiet you'd think the whole world had disappeared. A dragon slide looms over Triangle Park and there's a little brick church by the water whose sign suggests:

BELIEVE THE BEST
ABOUT JESUS

Never thought about it that way before. To give God and Jesus the benefit of the doubt, knowing they can't be as small and mean as we sometimes make them out to be.

Believing that Jesus really is good and that he loves me and wants to be my friend. That God isn't mad all the time, frustrated over how much I screw up, just waiting to pull the lever and drop me through the trapdoor to the flames. That God is not only merciful and graceful—he is Mercy and Grace, and if there are boundaries and restrictions it's because he wants what's best for me. Holding fast to the hope that true love never dies. Trusting that God hears the lowest cry and somehow, some way, has a plan to make everything turn out right.

I like that part in the Bible that says Jesus believes the best about me. That even though he can see all the movies that play in my mind, all that ugly secret junk I try so hard to hide—even knowing full well I am one wrecked and dirty treasure—he still decides I'm worth the effort to save. Believing that he works and searches out that secret best of me, even if it is the tiniest .001 percent of who I am. That God can take that tiny bit and grow it into something good.

I park at the shoulder and walk over to the church sign, just so I can see it up close. There's a fog hovering over the water, rising in a spiral through the trees. I sit back against the bricks and consider it all. Faith, hope, and wonder. Everybody believing the best, working together for the good.

Someday God and I will pedal slow and coast down the long, flat streets that wind by the lake in the suburbs of heaven, lights in the trees and stars on the water, and no time there—none at all. A place where it is perpetually now. And God will laugh and explain this business of life and death to me. But that won't take long. Then he'll tell me of everything now and everything new. I hope God thinks of these things—all-knowing, ever-present, personal God, First and Last, Creator of all things. I hope that he thinks of me as he oils and tightens the bike chains and looks forward to that day.

TWENTY-EIGHT
JESUS LAUGHS (I HOPE)

*"You can't take things too seriously
or it doesn't pay to live."*

–JOEY RAMONE

FOR YEARS I'VE PROWLED THE NIGHT, AND CHANGING MY sleep schedule has proven tough. I've got a bad case of bedhead, my clothes are rumpled, and in general it looks like I just woke up. Garrett passes me in the hall of the counseling center. "What happened to *you*?"

"I just woke up."

"It's nearly 1:00 p.m."

"Yeah," I answer blankly.

"Is that why you keep your office so dark? So you can steal a nap during sessions?" he says with a laugh.

"Ha, ha," I reply.

A beanpole kid with rabbit cheeks and too-big clothes fidgets just outside my door. "Hey, buddy," I say, sliding my arm around his shoulders. "You here to see someone, my man?"

"Her *name* is Amanda," the mother says stiffly.

Amanda bursts into tears.

I'm mortified and fumbling as Ginny, the therapist one door down, rolls out in her sporty, custom-made wheelchair to save the day. "Ignore him, honey, he's been hit in the head a lot. Come on back, let's talk."

I slink away and scan the lobby's couches for my first appointment. A woman with faraway eyes sits next to a man gripping a balled-up Bass Pro Shop hat, nervously working fringes into the brim. We exchange uncertain glances before I introduce myself and usher them to the back.

I hate couples.

Fifty long minutes later, I slip back through the lobby and into the front office. "I'm going to work at the Christian *Television* Counseling Center," I proclaim to Tink, the office manager, a five-foot fireplug honey of a gal, wholly devout with a wicked sense of humor. "I would much rather wave my coat jacket at people and slap them on the forehead. Anything other than being trapped in a room with some bickering, miserable couple for an hour that never seems to end."

"Mmm hmm," Tink says, digging through her purse for chapstick. "Your three o'clock is here."

I yank a tissue from the box on her desk and drape my tone with drama. "For your love gift of twenty dollars or more you'll receive this *limited-edition* miracle prayer cloth, which will ease and enable you through all sorts of trials, tribulations, and dastardly marital maladies. *Act now!* And gain defeat over depressions, delusions, drug addictions, and nighttime enuresis . . ."

Tink grins and gestures through the sliding glass. "Three o'clock," she says. "Right there."

Out in the waiting room stands a goofus-looking guy in cutoff slacks and a white wifebeater. An army cap sits sideways on his head; wires from his pocket stream tunes into his skull. He's throwing abstract gang signs and doing a little side-step jig while the gray-haired woman on the couch thumbs through *Guideposts* magazine and casts him wary glances.

"What's his story?" I ask.

"Dad's a pastor. Says the boy is 'purty near worthless.' Not working, dropped out of college. Plays in a band. We had him in youth group; he's a sweet kid, just being a kid. Dad's—" Tink severs the air with a chop of her hand.

"At least this is more my speed." I gather his papers and head for the door. "I'm taking this dude to play Putt-Putt."

"Have fun," Tink says.

Once in my office he opens his eyes wide to adjust to the lack of light and gazes around at my collection of oddball trinkets and surrealist synagogue fashion. "Hey man, have a seat," I greet him, slipping into the deep, green pleather of my chair.

"This a church deal, or what?" he asks, backing into the corner of the couch.

"Well, theoretically, you come in here, we close the door, and you can be who you really are. You don't have to act like you got it all together."

"No preachin', huh?" he asks.

"Nah. You get amnesty in here."

He turns his cap backward and laughs. "All right, then."

"That wasn't too bad, huh?" Tink says when we're done.

"Yeah, he was pretty cool," I answer. "What's next?" She raises her eyebrows and points through the window.

There's a doughy boy hiding behind the lobby's ficus, the

sparse fronds offering little camouflage. His arms are crossed, his face in a big, whiny pout. The mother shifts on her heels and clutches her purse before her. "Here he is," she says, as if she has brought me a darling new puppy to housebreak. "Talk to him!"

"What's his name?"

"Raymond."

An eight-year-old named Raymond? No wonder. I walk over and offer my hand. "Raymond, what's wrong?"

He wipes his sleeve across his face and glares at his mother. "This ain't Dairy Queen!"

I turn to her and crook my finger. "You lied to your kid about ice cream just to get him to come?"

"I had to," she explains.

"What did you think was gonna happen when you got here?"

"They said you might have some puppets or something?" she says meekly.

"Lady, I ain't Kermit the Frog. Take your kid to Dairy Queen."

After a brief squabble the woman grabs young Raymond by the wrist and steers him out the door. "Come on," she says, glowering back at me. "Let's go get your *ice cream.*"

Back in the front office, Holly the counseling intern smiles sweetly.

"I have a confession," I blurt out. "I do this because they pay me. I feel no spiritual calling or responsibility in the least. I do it for the money."

"Oh-kay," she replies. "Anything else?"

"I don't even really *like* people that much. People get on my last nerve."

"Got it," says Holly. "Feel better?"

"I guess," I answer as she places the phone in my hand.

Old Felton's voice crackles over the line from the church-sponsored secondhand store on the other side of the street. "There's a crazy girl on drugs or something over here and she won't leave. Can you send someone to get her out?"

"What's that you say?" I reply to Felton, locking eyes with Holly and flashing a maniacal smile. "You need someone to come get some drunk chick out of the thrift store? Oh, certainly. I'll be right over."

"Have fun," Holly chirps.

"Your day's comin'," I call back.

I head out the door and across the street. Once inside the store I pass by racks filled with cracked Flintstones glasses, crusty stuffed animals, and pictures of Christ that give me the creeps. I'm eyeing a magnificent cross-stitch of Bee Gees Jesus at the Last Supper when Felton cranes his head around the corner and waves me back.

There's a little crowd of people, some openly staring and others, well, staring not as obviously, peeping from the corners of their eyes while casually browsing the half-off culottes. Felton pushes up his glasses and gestures to the blonde babbling nonsense and tearing out pages from the Christian romance paperbacks. She's got Medusa hair, lime-green genie pants, and a purple sweatshirt that says PARTY HARD. (On the back: *Youth Group Lock-In Party like it's 1999.*)

As I step toward her, she drops and begins a furious set of sit-ups, from stretched back flat to leaning forward to grab her toes, six inches of threadbare underwear flashing from the back of her baggy pants. The customers slowly move their stares over to me.

I flop down beside her and start crunching. If nothing else, I am a faithful absurdist.

"What?" Medusa says defensively, watching me match her moves. The culotte shoppers have now forgotten their pants and stand in the aisles, eyeing us like hungry monkeys watching a clown juggle bananas.

"What?" I answer back. "A man can't work some abs at the thrift store?"

"What's your name?" she demands with a big nutty laugh. "I wanna know your whole life story. Don't leave not one thing out."

"You first," I tell her. "But we'll have to go back to my office."

She follows me over and stops a Cablevision van by doing a hoodoo dance in the street. "No time," I say, dragging her by the arm.

"Let her dance!" the Cablevision man yells from the van window.

I pull her through the parking lot and into the lobby. She excuses herself to the bathroom and stays way too long. I send in Holly to bring her out and we hustle her into my office.

"Look, I ain't gonna lie," Medusa says, cramming a fistful of Doritos into her mouth. "I just took a bunch of pills and shot-gunned a beer."

"Pills to overdose?" I ask. "Or just get high?"

Her eyeballs jangle like the cherries on a slot machine. "Fuzzled the eff up," she replies, raising one finger, then two. "S'cuse my French."

I shrug and she holds out her palm to high-five. "You're one of them churchies that's heard it all. That's cool. I can't look at you too long though 'cause I'm a sex addict." She turns to Holly and sadly shakes her head. "Can't look at you too long neither, babycakes."

"Sex addict?" asks Holly.

"Tried goin' to that support group thing y'all have." Medusa nods. "But everybody was hooking up so bad I had to quit."

"Ohh," Holly groans.

"Oh," I repeat.

On the side of her backpack is a blown-up color copy of her driver's license. The photo is of a sun-kissed girl with long, loose curls the color of champagne; her head is tilted back, eyes smiling and full of life.

"Crystal?" I read from the pack. "That's you, right?"

Her face goes dark. "I'm Crystal. But that's not me." She chokes a bit, her words warble. "Not anymore." Tears well up; she lifts her shirttail and wipes her face. There is a long silence while she cries, T-shirt raised and dabbing at her eyes, exposing her whale-white belly and tragic brassiere. I look to the wall and pray for poise. There are two tiny pictures of Jesus tacked behind my bookcase, one laughing, the other rolling his eyes.

Little help here, Jesus.

Finally Holly speaks. "What can we do for you, honey? Tell us what you need."

Crystal rolls up her chip bag, brushes her hands over my couch cushions, and lets out a deep sigh. "I don't know. The Lord, I guess?" She reads our faces a moment before adding, "And a hundred and fifty bucks for a bus ticket back to California." She turns to me. "And will you call my probation officer and tell her I came to counseling?"

Garrett taps on the door and motions me to the hall. "What are you going to do with the girl?" he asks.

Christ walked on water. Peter and Paul brought the dead back to life. Judas stole money and hung himself from the tree. James and

John were called twin sons of Thunder. Thomas refused to believe until he had seen the nail prints in Jesus' hand.

"I don't know."

"Anything I can do to help?" he says.

"Can you get me a hundred and fifty dollars?"

Garrett pauses, probably waiting for me to say I'm only kidding. "Make it two," I add.

"Give me thirty minutes," he says.

I slip back into the office. Holly and Crystal have their heads bowed in prayer.

". . . and God, just let Crystal know that you are always with her, help her to find her way and have peace in her heart and mind, amen."

"Amen to that," says Crystal, wiping away tears. She stands, stretches, and when she smiles, for a moment looks a little like the girl in the picture again.

"Sister Crystal," I say. "If you're goin' back to Cali, we might be able to help."

"You can?" she says, astounded. "I knew somebody was sending me over here today. You guys are like, saving my life."

I point to Holly. Holly points to me. Both of us point to Jesus.

"You really think Jesus laughs and rolls his eyes?" Crystal asks, in a hopeful kind of way.

What I really want to say is that I hope he does, that Jesus laughs because he knows we are blood and dirt made spirit by the work of his hands. Because laughter is the living essence of mercy and hope. I don't know why we are all such a mess behind the scenes, why life and religion and relationships can drive us so completely insane. The Bible is full of Jezebels and perverts and Peeping Toms and people who just can't seem to get it together no matter how hard they try. I hope those parts are there to remind us that God is good, grace trumps sin, and mercy stretches from sea to endless sky. That if Jesus laughs it's to help us not feel so messed up and alone, and to give us hope that somehow everything will be all right.

But I can't quite figure out how to put that into words. So I just shrug and give her a goofy smile.

"Hope so," I tell her. "I really do."

TWENTY-NINE

HANDSHAKES AND SIDE HUGS, THAT'S ALL

"Treat the young women like sisters."

–PASTOR REDDY'S PARAPHRASE OF 1 TIMOTHY 5:2

THERE'S THIS GIRL FROM CHURCH, BROOKE. SHE HAS long, blonde hair, a winning smile. I call her Brookie. She was a missionary to South Africa for several years, business major now. Sings for the contemporary service on Sunday mornings. We worked on a project together to help runaway kids, and lately we've been hanging out here and there. It's nice to have someone to pal around with. Even if she does talk a lot.

"Jamie," Brookie says as we pedal through the steam yard at the old water plant, "do you think God cares about our dreams? Whether we're really happy or not?"

"What do you mean?"

"Don't you ever just think about stuff? I mean, there's so much that you want to do and feel like you're supposed to do . . . but there's no way to do it all, you know? I'm scared sometimes

I'll make the wrong choices and mess everything up. But don't you think God will help us not to miss what he wants us to do? I know things happen for a reason, but do you ever just wonder how your life is going to turn out?"

"Sometimes."

"It's like, I know I'm supposed to go back to the mission field," Brookie continues. "I *know* that."

"Uh-huh."

"But I also know I want to have kids and be married and I dream about living in this big old white house up on a hill someday. With enough land to breathe but still be close to family and work and church and everything."

"That'd be nice," I reply.

We ride for a while, silent, coasting lazy arcs through towering rows of sky-blue pipe.

"How about you, Jamie?"

"How about me what?"

"You know," she says. "Hopes and dreams and stuff. What do you want to do someday?"

Guess I'm more used to listening than talking back. Kinda unusual having someone ask.

"I dunno."

I fall in behind her as we steer down a narrow walk that runs between the factory walls and tall panes of antique glass. A slender, brick smokestack blocks the moon. There's a break in the security fence where we can slip into the inner yard.

"Why are you so secretive?" Brookie says.

"What are you talking about?"

"You hardly ever talk about yourself. It's like I know you, but I don't really know you at all."

"What do you want to know?"

"I don't want to have to *ask*," she says as we slow the pace. "Just regular conversation? The way normal people talk?" She stares at me, waiting. I stare back, a little uneasy until she breaks the silence with a smile and sparkle in her eyes. "Call me curious, that's all."

"Hopes and dreams and stuff," I reply. "You really wanna know?"

Brookie nods her head. "Really," she says.

"I want to ride bikes through the old abandoned waterworks and out across the golf course. Stop and skip a few rocks across the pond on the seventh hole. Then maybe we could get an ICEE."

"But that's what we're doing right now."

"Yeah," I tell her. "Sometimes dreams come true."

The golf course lies beyond the giant culvert that cuts through the hillside. There's a big black willow blooming over the pond, embers flickering where fireflies hover at the water's edge. A thousand shades of night surround us, moonlit silver fading to gray, sepia giving way to dark shadows, clusters of indigo forest and long fairways of manicured grass.

"So that's it?" she asks. "That's all you want?"

There's this trick I used to do with my best buddy Ash during the summers of junior high. We'd ride side by side, let go of the handlebars, and grab on to each other's hands. See who could stay up the longest without pulling away. As we pedal along, I drift in close to Brookie and stretch out my hand. She wobbles at first then steadies and reaches back to lace her fingers through mine. On the count of three we release the bars.

"Jamie," she laughs, as we slip through the tunnel toward the dogleg on the sixteenth hole, "you are a strange one."

BROOKIE'S A REALLY GOOD-HEARTED GIRL. HER LIFE IS AN open book. She's attractive, well-adjusted, and focused on who she is and where she's going. Church relationships are weird because people don't want to just let you be friends. Church folk love to matchmake. But it's handshakes and side hugs whenever we part ways so we're just friends. Right?

"Do you think about her when she's not around?" Terry asks while we're walking the psych ward courtyard one night.

"I don't know," I hedge. "Sometimes? Not really, I guess."

"Then you're just friends," Terry says, shaking his head and stubbing out his Winston. "That's all."

"Yeah, I s'pose so. It's confusing, man."

"Pray about it, Jamie," Terry suggests. "Pray about everything. God has ways of letting you know where he wants you to be."

I'M MORE TORN THAN I LET ON. THERE'S THIS PRESSURE TO get your life together. To figure out your purpose and place before it's too late. It's tempting to let others decide the path for you. Easier. There's security in the conventional path. And the righteous path in this small Southern town is to find a steady job with benefits, get married, have kids, and park yourself in a like-minded group.

Hurry up already. What's wrong with you?

Sometimes I wonder what the people's reaction would be if Moses went to my church. I'm not sure what they'd think about all that wandering around in the desert. *Moses, you'd better get with Jesus and a map and find yourself the shortest, straightest line to your destination.* Not sure how King Solomon would fare either with all his talk of smoke in the wind and how meaningless everything seems. Oof, Jonah. *Get it together, boy.*

It'd probably be me, Jonah, Moses, and Solomon sneaking in late to the back pew. I hope there's enough grace to reach the back pews too. To be on the safe side, I've been sitting with Brookie closer to the front. Not the *front* front. But closer.

Sure enough, the closer you get to the pulpit, the friendlier people seem to be. Women come up, shaking our hands and looking back and forth from me to Brookie, saying, "Well, well, so *nice* to see you two today." Sit with a girl in church and pretty soon they've got you registered at Babies "R" Us.

Really, it's not so bad. Kinda nice to fit in. But now and then I can't help glancing toward the back. Moses rolls his eyes and Jonah's just staring at the ground. That wry smile slips across Solomon's face as he slowly shakes his head. There's a fourth guy back there but I can't quite catch his eye. Just my imagination, I'm sure. I should probably stop looking back.

THIRTY

ONE OF US

"There's really only you and me.
And it's always now."

–WILLIE NELSON

SKEETER IS HAGGARD AND LEAN, SHIRT HALF TUCKED
and hand-me-down dress pants covered with mud. He reeks of
cheap liquor and old sweat and speaks with the kind of lazy
Southern drawl that makes every sentence sound like a com-
mercial for hot grits and homemade biscuits.

"Why they call you Skeeter?" I ask.

"'Cause I can live right up in the thick of 'em and they don't
even bite me."

Skeeter drops into the church outreach now and then, telling stories and lies and outright nonsense at times about how he
thinks his daddy might be Webb Pierce, and that he once rode
in that Cadillac covered in silver dollars a long, long time ago.
He says if he just had some money for a DNA test he could prove
that silver-dollar car rightfully belonged to him.

"One day I'm gonna git it," Skeeter tells me. "And when I do, I'm gonna pick you up and we'll drive all over town so everybody can kiss our behinds."

"Shotgun," I declare. "I'm there."

Skeeter never asks for anything but accepts offerings gracefully and with thanks, some pots and old clothes, beans and rice from the church pantry. Recently, the deacon who owns the sporting-goods store donated a brand-new tent, and another set him up with an appointment to get his teeth fixed.

"I been to y'all's house. You oughta come see mine sometime. Don't nobody ever come see me," he says. "Got a nice little spot out by the bridge."

"Heck, yeah," I tell him. "I'll come."

Just over the hill from the boat landing, Skeeter's got a camp in the middle of a pine thicket. It's a tight circle of trees that offers solid protection, low profile, and a good vantage point to see out without being seen. When I get there he's poking at the coals with a long stick, trying to get a fire going again.

"C'mon in," he greets me. "Welcome to my humble abode."

A military tarp is draped over some low limbs and fastened with rope. The ground is cleared out underneath and there's a sleeping bag, kerosene lantern, and some paperback books filed side by side in a crate. I spot Merton, Lucado, and a large-print *Purpose Driven Life*.

"Good book," I say, pointing it out.

"I love books," he replies, ripping a few pages from the Lucado and feeding them to the edges where the cinders still seethe. I start to snicker but he rubs his hands together and warms them over the rising flame. Maybe he's just telling it straight.

"Hey," I say, helping stack fresh wood onto the fire. "I thought the church gave you a tent."

"They did," he says, reaching to the shadows and holding up a bottle. "I sure did appreciate that brand-new tent." He unscrews the lid and takes a nip.

I laugh now and tell him about the time I ran away from home and slept in the woods in my Hot Wheels sleeping bag, building a pine-straw fire and waking up blind and miserable because the smoke had been blowing in my face all night. He nods like he's been there and then, without taking his eyes off the fire, hands me the bottle.

I take it and feel its weight in my hand, the curve of the glass. "Hiram Walker Sloe Gin. Premium Mixer," the label says. There's a picture of some grapes. Skeeter waits, watching now.

If it gets back that I had a drink with the homeless guy, well, it might not look too good at the church. *Would Jesus drink from Skeeter's bottle?* I can see it either way. I can't always figure out what Jesus would do. Maybe he would perform some kind of miracle and make everything different somehow. Maybe Jesus would tell Skeeter about new wine and the kingdom and how there was plenty of room for him there. But God walking this planet as a man was always about people over rules. So I figure Jesus just might drink from Skeeter's bottle too. And if I'm wrong? Better to err on the side of grace.

I take a short pull. The flavor goes down harsh and sweet, then a burst of warmth radiates like a depth charge through my chest.

"Forgot how good sloe gin is on a cold night," I say, passing the bottle back.

"Sloe gin's good any night," Skeeter shoots back with a black-gapped grin.

"First thing I ever got buzzed on was sloe gin. I was thirteen. We were playing the Christmas parade and another drummer snuck a flask out from his old man's stash. We hid behind the 7-Eleven Dumpster with some girls from the clarinet section and drank sloe gin and Sprite during the fireworks show."

"Thirteen," Skeeter says. He fastens the top back and slides the bottle into the brush. "Tell you what happened to that tent y'all got me, if you really wanna know."

"Oh," I say, a little caught off guard. "Okay, sure."

He pulls out a cell phone and holds it to his ear. "Y'all at the underpass?" he says. "Wook and them down there?"

Skeeter leads me through a path near the tree line, the moon a gleaming crescent above, our breath a fog.

The trees give way to a Stonehenge-looking set of low concrete walls at the river's edge. Three men stand around a fire built in a barrel, hands jammed down into the pockets of their army jackets. They look past Skeeter to me and get quiet, their eyes bright in the flame.

"Who you got there?" the tallest man asks Skeeter.

"I seen you before," another man says. "One of them church folk."

"Him?" says Skeeter, as if he's forgotten I tagged along. "Naw, he ain't one of them . . . ." He loops his arm around my neck and laughs. "Ol' Hot Wheels here, he's more like one of us."

The tall man steps up, looking like a cross between Larry Bird and Willie Nelson with his braids down. "Preacher, 'preciate you comin' out here," he says, sticking out his hand. "Been wantin' to meet you. Everybody round here calls me Wookie."

THIRTY-ONE

SAVE A STAR

*"When it gets dark enough
you can see the stars."*

–CHARLES A. BEARD

WOOKIE STANDS AND WAVES LONG BEFORE I STOP THE truck. Scrawny white arms flap from a sleeveless tee, crude ink tattooed up and down his spindly limbs. Flames and skulls, names of long-lost girls. Lonesome Jesus.

He called me at the church a few hours before, asking for a ride from the grocery store to his new campsite. Said he got kicked out of the boarding house and chased from beneath the bridge by the FBI. Stayed awhile at Snake's house but then them crackhead women came over and he didn't want to be around none of that. Found a site out on Lake Felkell for only seven dollars a night. Just needs a ride.

"Hey! Hey brother!" he calls from just outside the store's front door, sacks of groceries stacked around his feet. I pull over, pop the lock, and Wookie hustles his grub inside. He's covered in flashy jewelry, and with his mossy hair and Manson beard he resembles a caveman rapper from the dirty South.

"What's all this?" I ask, shielding my eyes.

"My lady over to the pawn shop gives me all the broken necklaces and stuff and I fix 'em up to sell." He fingers a thick cross, crusted with fraudulent jewels, holding its bling to the light. "You want this one? It's white gold, good stuff."

"No, I can't take your cross; you keep it."

"I'll get you another one. What you like?"

"Something small."

"I'll do it," he says. "I'll get you one tomorrow."

"No rush." I dip into my T-shirt and pull out my gunmetal rosary, tempered with patina and time. "I got one."

He studies the beads, the crucifix in the dark. "That's a serious cross there. You Catholic?"

"I'm everything," I tell him. "I want all the good."

"Everything." He ponders and nods. "I like that. Me too. I want all the good I can get."

"Where'd you come up with grocery money?" I ask, pointing to his bags in the backseat.

"Cuttin' grass," he answers. "Got some lawns I keep over off Luster Lane."

I do some mental figuring. "That's ten miles from here."

"Yessir," he agrees. "'Bout twelve by bike."

"How you get your lawn mower over there?"

"Drag it behind the bike," he says.

I'm searching for the right reply to the idea of towing a lawn mower twelve miles behind a ten-speed bike when he jerks forward and knocks on the glass.

"Right here—right there by that RV." We turn into a dead

end, a black-and-tan mutt barking angrily in my high beams. "Nope, un-uh," he says, "ain't it."

Seven or so wrong turns later we find the dirt path down to the lake where his gear is set up. Tent next to a picnic table. Electric outlet and grill, fire pit on a slab overlooking the water.

"I like this," I say, telling the truth, not just being kind. "It's really peaceful out here."

"Yeah man, I love it. I got my sobriety, my serenity, and my God."

"Good place to be."

A drake drops from the sky to light on the lake's surface. The reeds part and a gander paddles over; they swim together in lazy esses. Wookie speaks low. "Figure this might be as good a place as any to finish."

The words come out of the blue, so I wait.

"Doc at the VA's been runnin' buncha tests," he says, staring into the stars on the far side of the water. "They ain't said it outright yet but I can tell."

"Finish," I repeat.

"You know," he says softly. "Finish."

Sometimes the night seems so infinite as if to eclipse any pain, as if the nature of all things is phases, circles, and cycles, one door closing only for another to open again. You think about these things listening to a zillion-cricket army singing harmony through the trees, standing under endless stars and the outstretched arms of galaxies. But somewhere between inner and outer space is the place where we live, and it seems a little silly to say such things out loud.

"Peaceful out here," I tell him again.

There's a trail across the water where the goose and mallard weave. Then the grey bird spreads his wings, rising back into the night. And the gander sits, still as a stone.

"Brother," Wookie says, resting his hand on my shoulder.

"Yeah?"

"That tent I got me is one bad lil' sonofabuck.Wanna see it?"

"You bet."

"I mean it's a, uh, real nice tent." Big smile. "Sorry, Preacher."

"S'okay," I tell him as we duck through the flap and step inside. "I'm not a preacher."

With a nod, Wookie laughs and rolls on. "Got cup holders in the sides and come with a sleeping bag and two pillows. Look here," he says, holding out his long, skinny arms. "Big 'nuff to stand up in. Eighty bucks brand-new. And Skeeter just give it to me, pretty much. Can you believe that?"

"All a man needs right here," I reply.

We step back out of the tent and stand there surveying the land. "Here, lemme give you some gas money for comin' get me," he says.

"No sir, thanks though."

"Aw, come on, I know that gas is high."

"Next time."

"Stay then, have a hamburger with me."

A rabbi in rehab for pain pills once taught me that those in need sometimes need to give back, to keep their self-respect. "That sounds good."

Wookie's eyes light up. "You hungry?" he asks.

"Sure am."

"Got a hobo special for you," he says after the burgers are done. Wookie layers a thick piece of government cheese onto the meat, stacks potato chips onto two slices of white bread, and smushes it all together flat with the palm of his hand.

"Here ya go, brother," he says, handing me a paper plate and ducking his head. "God bless, thanks, that's grace."

"Amen," I reply.

We sit there on the bank eating hobo burgers while the steady murmur of TV news bleeds over from a trailer down the lane. Wookie shifts his food to the side of his mouth and traces the arc of a star falling over the waters.

"Know what that is?" I ask.

"Falling star?" he says.

"Actually, I majored in astronomy for a while," I tell him. "That's Enoch's chariot going home."

"Enoch who?" he asks.

"Enoch in the Bible. Enoch was, then he was not," I answer. "For God took him and he arrived. Enoch was a friend of God."

Wookie watches the sky with awe, as if what I've told him about stars falling is gospel truth.

"Hey Jesus," he says low. "Save a star for me."

———

I LIKE TO THINK I WOULD'VE BEEN THAT ONE GUY WILLING TO stay awake and talk to Jesus all night in the garden. I don't think I would have been able to sleep. I may not have been the smartest apostle or the best studied or the guy with the most leadership skills, but I could have been that guy who stayed up with Jesus the night before he died. In fact, if I had my time machine, I'd go back and be that guy, and then you could read about me in the Bible.

But verily, there was this one sort of shaggy-looking guy who stayed awake with Jesus, and they sat there in the cool dark night and talked of faith and doubt and the strange nature of all living things. Sometimes, we heard them laugh.

That would be pretty cool to be mentioned in the Bible, especially if it were for something good and not for being a liar or a cheat or that backstabbing friend who ratted you out for some cash.

But I don't have a time machine. So I figure the best I can do is stay up and talk to Jesus now. I've never been good at a lot of church stuff. Church stuff is sort of like algebra to me. Most of the time, I just don't get it. I scrabbled my way through grad school so I don't know a lot of counseling skills either. It might sound goofy, but the only way I know to do any sort of counseling, crisis intervention, or outreach ministry, is to believe that I am going to hang out with Jesus.

Jesus said whatever you do for the least of my brothers and sisters, you do for me. So when I go see that guy in jail who is crying and kicking the wall, I think, *There's Jesus.* And if he's eating screws and he curses and throws his shoes at me, well, maybe it's more like, *Okay, that's Jesus' little brother. Still. Better be patient. Be kind.*

When I drive up at four in the morning to see some woman babbling to aliens and doing the tango hustle through her neighbor's yard with tinfoil wrapped around her head and no pants on, *There's Jesus.* Or at least his little sister. So find her some pants and bring her cold water. Sit on the back steps and listen to whatever story she needs to tell. Do the best I can to help her get from where she is to where she needs to be. Because someday

Jesus will meet me just outside the gate, and I don't think he's going to ask where I went to church or how many Bible verses I memorized. He's going to say, "Where were you when I was sick? When I was in jail? How about when I was hungry? Where were you when I lost my mind?"

I can't imagine that night in the garden, before he died, Jesus would have wanted to hear a bunch of religious encouragement. I don't think that he would have wanted me to pat him on the back and quote Philippians 4:13 or that verse that talks about plans to prosper and do no harm. I don't think Jesus would have wanted me to preach to him or tell him how he should feel. I imagine the best I could do was sit there with him through the night and listen and acknowledge that life can be pretty hard and confusing at times.

Sometimes I think the best ministry is to just be there. With no answers or agendas, willing to admit there are some things in life you can't fix or figure out. Makes things simpler if I look at it that way. I don't have to be good at systems and sermons or magic phrases and prayers. I don't have to be charming or motivational or articulate. All I have to do is be willing to show up and sit with Jesus.

THIRTY-TWO

STANDING ON THE HILLTOP WITH BOTH HANDS IN THE AIR

"Don't try so hard."

—AMY GRANT

THE MESSAGE ON THE CHURCH BIG SCREEN BURNS brightly: STOP GOING THROUGH THE MOTIONS. The letters fade slowly, one by one. A new message emerges in its place: START LIVING.

A stock picture appears on the Jumbotron: a woman on a hill with her hands lifted high. The words beneath her feet read, DISCOVER YOUR PURPOSE. A larger word surges, engulfing the woman and then the hill until it fills the screen: N O W.

"God loves busy hands," the preacher begins, holding out his palms. "God loves a busy mind," he adds as he paces back and forth across the platform. "And God loves those who are busy about the business of doing good." He pauses and points into the camera with an expert smile. "And all things work together for the good, for those who love God and are called according to his plan."

In this sermon series at church, the pastor talks about purpose and finding your place, following Christ and getting your act together. He preaches it well enough to make you feel sure, like you really could fix your life with a few simple steps and some prayers.

"Now I want to say something to you single men," the preacher says after the last of his four-point plan. It seems he is staring directly at me. "Women are attracted to success. A leader. A man of vision *focused* on discovering his perfect path. *Fixed* . . . on becoming the person God has called him to be." He pauses for effect, to let his message drift out over the room. "We need to be people of *purpose*," he insists. "Men of a serious mind."

I have no steady job, no benefits, no real savings of any kind. No real plans past the present. I'm spinning my wheels and living day-to-day with three part-time jobs that cover my basic needs with enough left over for Chinese food and Cocoa Pebbles now and then. I've got about two months' grace before I have to start paying back all those student loans I racked up goofing around in undergrad. Truck's getting old. My clothes are all ragged. How long can you stay up half the night, sleep till noon, and live in a pool house? Maybe it's time to quit goofing around.

But how do you know when it's time? When the roads dead-end and the walls close in? Change is good. Change is necessary. But you can't just change for change's sake, right? How do you really know?

The preacher steps down and stands at the altar. "Calling. Focus. Purpose. Plans," he says, hammering each point home with a rallying fist. "With heads bowed and no one looking around, if you would say to me, Pastor Mark . . . I need help in finding my way, in becoming the person I'm called to be. Because I don't want to miss one thing God has for my life. I've tried and tried but I just can't seem to be sure. I just can't seem to find it on my own. If that's you tonight, if you just want to be *sure* . . . I want you to lift up your hand so I can pray for you."

The sanctuary is silent, the pianist playing softly while we wait. I sit with elbows on knees, face to the ground. Surely hands are lifted across this room. *Who wants to miss their call? Who doesn't feel like they've fumbled and tried? Doesn't everybody want to find their place?* With every head bowed, I slip up my hand.

"Yes, brother. Yes," the pastor replies. "I see that hand."

WE'RE FRIENDS, REALLY. WE SIT TOGETHER AT CHURCH sometimes, eat Chinese. Ride around and talk now and then.

"Jamie," Brookie says, "do you want a boy or girl first?"

"Boy or girl what?"

"Kids, silly," she says, with a cluck of her tongue. "Boy first or a girl? Or does it matter?"

"Ah, geez, Brookie," I reply, rolling down the window to spit out my gum. "What are you talkin' about?"

"Why do you always call me Brookie and never Brooke?" she says. "Don't you call anybody by their real name?"

"All my friends have nicknames. That's how you know you're my real friend."

"Is that what I am?" she asks, sliding across the seat and pulling my hair back into a ponytail.

"What are you doing?"

"Seeing what you look like with short hair," she says. "It looks nice."

I pull free and shake my hair out until it hangs down over my face. "Back off, churchy girl," I tease.

She scoots back toward the door, glaring at the dash. "Jamie," she says. "Sometimes you act like you don't even care. About nothing."

"Of course I do."

"Yeah, but you try to act like you don't," she says, arms crossed across her chest. "You're so full of it sometimes."

The truck cab is tense now. Neither of us speaks. I drive faster until the rims begin to rattle. She sighs and uncrosses her arms. "You have so much going for you. I just hate to see you waste it."

We stare at passing street signs and the highway before us. I ease my foot off the gas until the needle drops back to twenty-five. "So you don't want kids someday?" she asks, in a sweeter voice now. "You'd be such a fun dad."

"I love kids. I've got a rink full."

"I mean your own."

"I don't know."

Brookie laughs a sad sort of laugh. "I don't know, I don't know," she says in a sing-song voice, wobbling her head back and forth. "One of these days, Jamie, you're going to have to know something."

"Yeah," I reply. "One of these days."

THERE'S AN ASSOCIATE PASTOR AT THE CHURCH I REALLY like, Brother Sammy, a big, broad guy who wears loud suit jackets and gets his hair cut at Fantastic Sams. He's been married nearly thirty years, attractive wife, kids grown and doing well. Sammy and Carol make a seemingly great team. I pray for a marriage like theirs someday.

Sammy lives just a few blocks over, so I'll stop by sometimes to shoot the breeze. But when I show up tonight his head is hung low, Carol's crying in the kitchen, and it's obvious they've been at war. I know all couples argue but it's shocking to see up close. I guess you figure the people who lead the marriage seminar at church shouldn't have problems. Sometimes I can still be so naive. I excuse myself and start to leave when Sammy motions for me to wait.

"Hold up, Jamie," he says, steering me toward the carport door. "You don't have to rush off, do you?"

The garage is dark, shadows and light spilling into the perimeter from the street. Brother Sammy is sitting on the washing machine and I'm leaning against the hood of his classic El Camino, midnight blue. Sister Carol took a sleeping pill and went upstairs to lie down. Truth is safer late in the night, and dark garages can be holy ground. So I sit back and listen, letting Sammy lead the way.

He talks about secret struggles and the pressure to put on a front, trying to hold on to what matters without losing who you are. About how confusing relationships and chemistry can be, how sometimes the person you marry changes, and quite honestly, time and circumstances change you too. Sometimes struggle and change bring you closer together and other times they drive you apart. One day you wake up miles away. I don't try to give him any advice. I just let him say whatever he feels like he needs to say.

"Wish we could talk more like this at the church," Sammy tells me after a while. "People need it."

"What about the other pastors?" I ask. "You guys don't talk?"

"Jamie, just because you're a good preacher, that doesn't necessarily make you a good man," he says. "A lot of pastors are just CEOs who know some Greek. You have to be careful what you say around there."

"Yeah, but why?" I ask. "That doesn't even make sense."

"Don't know," he says. "Somehow that's just the way it is."

There's a long, easy silence between us.

"Brother," I tell him. "I sure do love this car."

"Had one just like it in high school," he says, with a tone somehow both modest and proud. "Carol found me this one for my birthday last year."

"It's awesome."

"Come on, I'll take you for a ride," he says. "Tell you what. I'll even let you drive."

"No way."

"Way," he replies, tossing over the keys.

We motor up Seventh, turn left, and roll slow down Lilac Street. Elbow out the window, hand beating time on the side of the door as Steve Perry sings about love, loneliness, and living just to find emotion, streetlight people hiding in the night.

"So," Sammy asks while the lead guitar blisters. "What's going on between you and Sister Brooke?"

I reach over and turn the stereo down. "Brooke's a nice girl," I reply.

"She's precious," he says. "Listen son, just because relationships are difficult, that doesn't mean they can't be good."

"Yes sir," I tell him. "I know."

"But you have to work them out your own way. No one else can work it out for you."

There's a long train stopped at the crossing, a switcher working to couple the last two cars. Far away at the mill, a whistle blows. We cut down a side road that runs through thick forest, windows down, listening. Some birds sing only at night.

"Yes, sir," I say again. "I know."

THIRTY-THREE

BLACK BELT BIBLE MONSTERS

*"I've yet to meet someone who found
their way to faith by being criticized."*

–PHILIP YANCEY

"HEY SUPER BIBLE BOY," TAT JABS. "IF JESUS IS SO GREAT,
why are Christians so crazy?"

Tat from Kat, short for Katherine, and she's got an ink-black
buzz cut and a turquoise dragon tattooed up her back and over
the shoulder. She runs a funky little salon out by the bowling
alley. It's decorated with vintage horror schlock and rock post-
ers, and the music is always up loud—old punk and Waylon,
Ozzy and Peter Tosh. Because I work at the church, she calls me
Super Bible Boy. Despite that, I think she likes me.

"Turn. Or burn. Heathen," I drone, lurching toward her with
teeth bared.

She feigns a swoon and shrieks like Elvira. Then, in a growl
straight from the tagline of a Tarantino film, "Black Belt Bible

Monsters Meet the Tattooed Hairdresser from Hell! Zombie Christians—trying to eat my brain!"

There's one other person in the shop, a gawky teenage girl wearing checkered tights and a denim miniskirt and sitting in the first chair. "He better not be too hungry then," zings the girl, guffawing like a cartoon donkey.

"Ooh," I say, giving her points for the slam.

"Shut it, you two," Tat threatens, wielding her clippers. "I'll skin you bald. The both of you."

Tat's mile-a-minute mouth knows no filter—UFO theories and unsolicited sexual advice—but she's interested, too, always asking about what music I'm into these days, how my job and love life are going, that kind of stuff. Her tattoos and attitude have given her a reputation around town, and I've heard rumors of everything from pill peddling to skinny-dip parties at the Texas Motel. But Tat doesn't seem to care what people say, and neither do I. She's cool to me and I like the way she cuts my hair.

I take the next chair over and wait while Tat smoothes the girl's newly black-and-white-streaked page-boy cut. "Looks hot, doll. Your parents know, right?"

"Yeah, uh? They said if I made straight As I could do whatever I wanted and they'd pay for it." The girl presses two twenties and a ten into Tat's hand.

"Congrats, sweetie," Tat says, slipping the twenties into her leopard-print blouse and sliding ten back toward the girl. "That's for the As. Go get a milkshake." She spins her around in the chair. "Hey Bible Boy," she says, "I present to you . . . Jilly Beanie, the Teenage Queenie! What do you think about this hair?"

"Your hair?" I reply. "It's *awesome.*"

"Yay!" Jilly cheers, tossing her new do around. "Hold out

your hand." I reach out until our palms and fingers press together. "Peace!" she declares, eyes squeezed shut. "I give you good energy."

"I receive it!" I respond. Jilly hugs Tat and hobbles toward the door, dragging a withered leg behind her.

"*Love* her," Tat mouths to me.

"What's wrong with her leg?"

"Born with it," Tat says. "But girl don't let it get her down."

Jilly Bean climbs into her tiny clown car and cranks the stereo, bass rattling the windows of the salon. As she pulls away she rallies her fist out the window and puckers her face into a menacing snarl.

We raise our fists in salute; Queenie eases into traffic, off and away.

"Geez. At her age I was knocked up." Tat sighs, her fingers through my hair. "Kicked out, livin' on my own. But things happen for a reason, you know . . ." She fans out her lime-green fingernails, tapping them against my head. "All right—still growing it out in front?"

"Long and low."

"Cool," Tat says, her ruby lips smacking gum. "Hey, you in a hurry?" I shake my head and she motions me to the back alley where she cowboy-straddles a kitchen chair and fires up a Lucky Strike. "I had this crazy dream the other night. Wanna hear it?"

"People always telling me their dreams," I say in a bogus grumble, "like I can decipher what they mean. I'm not a psychic— I'm a psychotherapist at a megachurch."

"Yeah, but you'll like this one. Jesus was there."

"Let's hear it."

She spins the chair around, sits forward, and sets the scene with her hands. "Okay, so a mob was chasing me through the woods. At night. I don't know why. In the distance, I see a man working through a shop window. Oil lamps were burning and everything was like, old—but new. I can't explain it. It was back then but right now, you know?"

"I dream that way too," I tell her. "Past and present all mixed up."

"So I banged on the window and yelled, '*Help!*'" she continues. "And he let me in. It was him."

Most everything in the alleyway is some shade of brick red or gray, flyers from a payday loan company scattered in dead grass, the dirt path between buildings spilling into a side street two spaces down.

"What'd he look like?" I ask, leaning closer now.

"Skinny with a beard. Kinda rough," she says, sitting back, lost in the dream. "And he smelled like sawdust and WD-40. I love that smell. I stayed there a long time, until the mob was gone. At the door as I was leaving he said, 'Katherine, you can hide here anytime.'"

"So what happened then?"

"He gave me his cell phone number."

"Jesus has a cell phone?" I ask.

"It was a dream, dude. But you know, I wouldn't tell this to just anyone—but that feeling stayed with me. It's the first time I'd thought of Jesus where he wasn't mad at me. He was nice. He said I could call him anytime."

A school bus passes, the tangle of voices louder, then fading away. Tat tilts her head to me. "You believe in dreams?"

"I don't know," I tell her. "What do you believe?"

She takes two pieces of her hair and twists them together

down the side. "Sometimes I feel like God and church and the Bible, like that stuff isn't for people like me. Like I'm too screwed up or somethin'." She sucks a good half inch off the cigarette; her smoke drifts through the air. "You know what I'm sayin'?"

"Tell you the truth," I say. "I don't believe real good a lot of the time either."

"I guess I believe a little," she says, holding her thumb and forefinger a hair's width apart. "Sometimes."

"Me too," I tell her. "A little. Sometimes. I think that's where we all start though."

"Hope so," she says.

Blackbirds light in the alley. A slow wind rustles the papers near our feet. Tat drops her cigarette and crushes it beneath her heel. "Let me show you something," she says, fumbling with the buttons of her blouse.

"Whoa, girl," I say, reeling back.

"No, silly," she laughs. "This. A new one." She points to a small tattoo near the bottom of her breastbone, a bearded man with eyes of piercing fire. "You know," she tells me. "They say this is where the heart really is."

I READ IN A BOOK THAT EVEN THINKING ABOUT GOD IS A form of prayer, and just about everyone I know says they think about God a lot. Lots of prayers in desperate hours, in the dead of the night when you just can't sleep. I don't know how God can seem so near and yet so far away at the same time. All I know is that in some perfectly imperfect way, this seems to be the universal path, the nature of all things—faltering through a fallen land, trying to minimize the damage and grasping for an unchanging hand that often seems just beyond reach, yet urging us on.

Jesus never turned anyone away who approached him honestly. He never manipulated or pushed anyone. He never sold one thing. He valued humanity, accepted people as-is, and said anyone, anywhere could be redeemed.

This is the way God came down to earth.

THIRTY-FOUR

CHRISTMAS CRAZY AT THE DOLLAR GENERAL STORE

"And He shall speak peace unto the heathen."

—HANDEL'S *MESSIAH*

IT'S THE NIGHT BEFORE THE NIGHT BEFORE CHRISTMAS.

"She didn't OD on much, but we gave her the charcoal hard," the nurse tells me. "She's a wreck but go on in."

I push through the ER doors and locate my charge. A girl sporting heavy makeup, black galoshes, and candy-cane stockings is puking furiously into a metal pan.

Her face is pasty, clothes covered in smudge. Ebony tresses streaked with green and red cascade from her head. An earring dangles; Jack the Pumpkin King from *The Nightmare Before Christmas*.

I take a seat and roll up to the bed.

"*BLARG!*" she hacks, her lock-and-chain necklace clanging against the stretcher's rail.

If I lower my head and pouf out my hair I can look a bit like Edward Scissorhands with Stallone in the lead. It's my best Goth move so I give it a shot, holding the pose until she looks up.

"*BLECH!*" she retches, toes curled, with a little convulsing writhe at the end. Middle finger crooked, she swabs a string of drool from her mouth and into the pan. She rolls over, arms splayed, and tries to catch her breath. Her violet-crusted eyes creep open and she spies me, watching like a crow.

"Merry Christmas," I say.

She laughs, a weak little sticky laugh, and curls into a ball. "Christmas sucks," she replies. "I hate it."

"No you don't," I tell her. "You love it too much and it lets you down. Lots of people feel that way."

"Christmas shouldn't be so hard," she says, just before gagging again. "God should call a truce or something."

I WENT TO A FAMILY CHRISTMAS GET-TOGETHER THIS afternoon and they didn't have any Diet Coke. They had *cola* but it was that off-brand, flat-tasting stuff—Dr. Packer or something like that—and I was in that frame of mind where your skin is crawling and you feel thirteen again, hormonal and alien, like everything's okay, but nothing is all right. So I snuck behind the nativity scene and huffed some kerosene from a paper sack.

Kidding. Actually, I just excused myself and drove to the corner store. But the J-Mart had chintzy fountain cokes with funky ice and not enough carbonation—the kind that makes you feel syrupy sick after you drink it.

I was in a black mood by the time we left for Christmas Eve service but then I thought of all the poor children, of the broken soldiers, of all the lonely, hungry, sad Christmas people with no family and friends. And now I'm in a bad mood for *being* in a bad mood, for not being grateful or gracious or capable of glad tidings and cheer.

We arrive late and the church is packed; the only seats available are in the middle of the second pew. Elbows and knees, we slide in as the house lights dim and a giant garland of sparkly lights glows from behind the pulpit. A mother-daughter duo take the stage to over-emote their way through the awkward carol "Christmas Makes Me Cry" as the congregation swoons.

Maybe it's because I've played with the kind of singers who can cut loose with a verse of "Jesus Paid It All" that would make Hitler weep, but it's all a bit much for me. Eyes crossed, I chime in on the bass part, a little flat. "Sometimes Christmas makes me craz-eee . . ." Sad glances are exchanged around me; no one is amused. Maybe it's just that I'm a cynical jackass lacking a true spirit of joy.

Broadway big, the duo's weepy carol ends and the cheerful flock rises to applaud. The pastor practically skips to the pulpit, clapping along; the people are seated and his message begins: "Some two thousand years ago, a child was born . . ."

I read a study the other day that said Halloween was now America's favorite holiday. Evangelicals might be quick to blame evil forces but scratch the surface and you realize it's probably because Halloween is all about fun and pretending with none of the emotional weight and sentimentality that family-based religious holidays hold. Family and religion make a lot of people very anxious. Don't get me wrong. I love Jesus and I love Christmas and sometimes it's amazing, but other times the holidays have got me a little crying and crazy too. All the restless thoughts, the accounting of another year's end.

Why are my relationships so strange and complicated?

What happened to my dreams?

What's wrong with me?

Expectations and emotional roller coasters. Longing for something magical, for beauty in a world of chaos, the secret wish that just for one day everything would be all right.

The girl at the ER was right. Christmas shouldn't be so hard.

I hit the side door and cut out early. It's the season of epiphany and mine is this: outside of grace and a wide comfort zone, I am rotten.

Dollar General is the only store open, so I pull into the lot for some rations. There's a ramshackle house not fifteen yards away; the front door opens as I step out of my truck.

A teenage couple argues on the porch. Just inside I can see a younger girl, fifteen maybe, bouncing a baby on her hip, silhouetted in the TV's light.

With a slam of the door, the couple rambles through the gravel toward the store. I walk in behind them and gather my things. Grape G2, a carton of eggs.

Tending the register is an effeminate fellow with a receding hairline and a rhinestone stud in his right earlobe. I pay. He grunts and moves my goods over the scanner and down to the end.

The young couple steps in behind me, loading their items onto the counter. Store-brand diapers. Ramen noodles. Few cans of tuna. The girl's hair is dark at the roots, straggling out into a matted mess the color of mozzarella cheese. Her breath is heavy with congestion, her eyes like glass. Skinny and pale with scattered acne and a shock of black hair, the boy hangs like a scarecrow behind her.

I watch them as I bag. His face strains with the math as their purchases are scanned. When the total flashes he pulls out four ones and some change, gives the girl a panicked look, and counts his change again.

I slide a ten to the cashier. "Here you go." I say this quietly, matter-of-fact.

The boy stares at the bill awhile before speaking. "We don't need yer fricken money."

His girl turns, her face sour. "What you think, we're trash or somethin'?"

The cashier glares as if I've offered kindergartners cocaine. I fumble, no words come.

"Go put them diapers back," she orders the boy. "I can get some from Mama in the mornin'."

"Okay, then," I say. I sweep up the ten, grab my things, and head out to the truck.

The younger girl waits in the front screen door, baby in her arms, watching for the couple's return.

"Hey," I call to her, "the cashier gave me too much change. You want it?"

Angling the baby inside, she cautiously looks me over. I stand with hands down and the most harmless look I can muster.

"It's Christmas," I say, holding out the money. "For baby."

She steps out and smiles. In the porch light she glows, awkwardly beautiful in an innocent sort of way. Her green eyes match the child's. "Heck yeah, I want it," she says.

I walk over and pass her a twenty through the porch rail. She turns it twice in her hand. "Wow," she says, pulling a strand of auburn hair from the corner of her lips. "What are you, an angel or somethin'?"

"Or somethin'," I reply.

We share a quick laugh before I leave. As I'm pulling away she takes the baby's arm and waves good-bye.

In the rearview mirror I see her do a bouncy little jig and hold out the bill as the couple climbs the steps. With a short bleat of the horn, I return the wave.

Some two thousand years ago a child was born
to a teenage girl on the poor side of town.
Dubious men arrived bearing gifts.
This is Christmas, the season of redemption and hope.

THIRTY-FIVE

DRIVE ON

"Somewhere ages and ages hence:
Two roads diverged in a wood."

—ROBERT FROST

I'M DRIVING DOWN RIVERSIDE IN A POURING, GRAY RAIN,
headed for home, turning things over in my mind. When you hear
so many stories, they start to run together into one big patchwork
quilt of mismatched pieces and frayed seams. You can't help but
wonder what it says about the state of all things, about church
and work and relationships and life on planet Earth.

It's tempting sometimes to sit in the counselor's position,
analyzing behaviors and playing the sage, like somehow I'm
above it all. But I am not above it. I'm frayed and mismatched
too. I am still so far from where I need to be.

I have committed theft, chased idols, and been guilty of both
murder and adultery in my heart. I have forgotten the Sabbath.
I've loved self far more than my neighbor or God. I have been

guilty of all these things since the hour I first believed. Sometimes I wonder if I even really believe at all.

I doubt too much. I think too much. Every time I try to be spiritually confident or cool, I put my foot in the mop bucket. Every time I think I've got it together, I lose it again. Sometimes I wonder if God just looks at me and shakes his head.

Sorry, Lord. Guide me, oh Mercy and Grace. Every day, trying to do a little better than the day before.

So it helps me to see firsthand that the church is constantly stepping in the mop bucket too. Truth is, I need to see that hypocrite guy who can't quite get his actions and beliefs on the same page. Smug little preachers and showboat singers and evangelism schemes that don't impress anybody outside the fold. Bandwagon mentalities and bait-and-switch sales pitches. Sappy songs and tacky T-shirts. All the distant, distracted, professionally religious and politely practiced church staff.

You see some nutty stuff working in a church—some really crazy people. But then, if you watch, you'll see some of those same crazy people do beautiful things. The arrogant deacon feeds the hungry, the hypocrite cares for the sick, the religious bigots band together to build some widow a wheelchair-accessible porch. And I realize that whether I am at a bar or a psych ward or a megachurch, people are just people; and in the dark, lonely places we're all basically the same, frightened and confused and feeling like we're doing the best we can.

Knowing that the beautiful, shiny, churchy people are just as messed up as the rest of us, well, it gives me a strange kind of hope. The feeling that maybe I can make it after all.

It helps me see that from Moses to John the Revelator, from Adam to the last man who will ever live, we are all screwups, stumbling through, lusting and loving and trying and killing and giving and living and dying and wondering why.

God in broken vessels, the Almighty come to earth as a man, misfit Jesus choosing that troublemaker Peter—of all people—to build his church upon. Jehovah the carpenter, the one they called Mary's illegitimate son, crucified between criminals and promising paradise to the thief who pleaded, "Remember me."

God help us all to laugh at ourselves and confess that the only thing we are sure of is how little we truly know. To admit that mercy, grace, hope, faith, God, and heaven had better be far bigger than we have made them out to be.

I love the crazy, beautiful, broken, busted-up church. But I wonder—should I really be working in one? Is it really the right place for someone like me?

There's a one-lane, cobblestone bridge that connects Madison to Ninth. It's a little out of the way, but I like to take it just to feel my wheels against the stone, to look out at the lights that line the water, reflecting back from the river's edge. Can't see the lights tonight. Nothing out the window but cold, gray sheets of rain.

The only conclusion I can come to is this: People are so crazy. Grace. People are so confused. Grace. People are so lost and lonely, even the church people, even the preachers, even the counselors. Even me. Grace.

For so many of the deep, true, difficult questions of life, there are no easy answers. Except for the hope that all roads lead to grace. And grace leads me home. And if all roads lead to grace, you have to drive on. Even if the road is narrow and you can't see the lights; even if the rain is cold and gray. That's what faith is—not knowing but still driving on. I can make it home from wherever the road takes me. I just have to drive on.

Up ahead in the distance there's a beacon that's brighter than the rain. Actually, it's just the Quik Stop. But a peach ICEE sure would be good right now. Heard they got in a new pinball machine. Be nice to stop by and kick back awhile.

The traffic light ahead flashes yellow as I push the accelerator to the floor. From the corner of my eye I spot the speeding car. I fumble for the brake and then the gas. Tires slide on slick pavement into a sickening thud, twisted metal and shattering glass. Everything fades to black.

"I THINK I'M ALL RIGHT," I TELL THE FIREMAN. "AM I ALL right?" He touches just over my ear and shows me the blood. I stagger over and sit on the curb, waiting for a ride to the ER. A bus full of band students passes with the windows cracked and they laugh. The wrecker comes and unlashes the winch. The Trooper is smashed, front end mangled and the radiator split, her right headlight gouged out and hanging to the side. Oil leaks into the street, shimmering as it snakes toward the drain. A man in blue coveralls hooks a chain to the axle and hauls the carcass up to his truck. Shards of metal spark against the pavement as he slowly drags her away.

"Any previous concussions?" the ER doc asks as he stitches the gash.

"A few," I reply.

"How many?" he asks.

When I answer he shakes his head. "Slow it down, son," he says. "You really can't afford any more."

The desk clerk enters and asks for my insurance card. "Don't have one," I tell her. "I think that other lady. She hit me."

"The police will determine who was at fault," the clerk frowns. "If you don't have insurance, you will be responsible for today's bill."

"Whoa, okay," I reply, a little woozy still. I open my wallet and show her the five and four ones inside. "You guys need me to pay something now?"

"No, no," she says. "We'll send you a bill."

"For how much?"

"You're probably looking at about four grand."

The doctor's balding with glasses, gray hair around the sides. He ties off the last stitch and stands. "A little water won't hurt but keep it clean," he says, shining his tiny light in my eyes. "If you get dizzy or start throwing up, be sure to come back, okay?"

"Will it be another four grand?" I ask. "'Cause I can get dizzy and throw up at home."

"Seriously," he says, clicking off the light. "You got somebody to look after you tonight? Make sure you're okay?"

"Yes, sir," I tell him. "I'll be fine."

I walk out front and look around the downtown streets. No angel cabs in sight. A battered old pay phone sits at the far end of the parking lot, its panel light flickering and dim. Seems suitably dramatic for such a night. So I walk over, pick up the receiver, and slip in some change.

I dial the first three numbers. *It's really late.* Hang up. Jesus needs a cell phone. *Where are you tonight, Jesus?* Start over again, dialing the first six, my finger hovering over that one last nine. *Just call her.*

A van with the hospital logo pulls up beside me with the window down. There's a grizzled old guy smoking a cigar at the wheel. "Hey, buddy," he says. "You need a ride?"

I nod, hang up the receiver, and reach for the sliding side door. "Up front," he says. "You can ride up here."

I walk around and climb in on the passenger side. "Are you the angel?" I ask. Still woozy, I guess.

"I ain't no angel," he says, chewing the cigar and steering back onto the road. "But I can get you home."

The van is warm and dry, tires humming over slick city streets. *Four grand. Purpose, calling, and plans. No-shows, cancellations. Student loans coming due. Stitches. Spinning wheels.* My chin drops to my chest, eyes shut.

"Wake up, buddy," the driver says, reaching over to shake my arm. "You gotta stay awake."

THIRTY-SIX

HEAD DOWN, DO RIGHT

*"Beware of all enterprises that
require new clothes."*

–THOREAU

IN A WINDOWLESS FEDERAL BUILDING, I REPORT TO A small office on the third floor. The room smells like burnt coffee and copy toner. No pictures. No calendar. No quips or quotes or plaques of affirmation. Everything is state regulation and gray. Behind the desk sits a serious woman in black slacks, flats, and hose with rips at the ankle.

"Mr. Blaine," she says, shaking my hand like a man. She looks like John Goodman saddled with a bad perm and chronic back pain. There's a half-eaten bag of microwave popcorn and stacks of files on her desk. A moldy stain sweats from the ceiling down the wall. Asbestos, I presume.

"The position," she says, reading from the page: "Case worker for court-ordered counseling, alcohol and drug treatment, anger management, and family-liaison work. Forty weekly hours, rotate call on nights and weekends. Starts at fourteen twenty-five hourly with benefits after ninety days. Two weeks of yearly vacation. Have you ever worked with offenders before?"

"Yes ma'am," I reply. "You could say that."

She rustles through the popcorn and reads the rest of the description to herself. My foot bounces with nervous energy, so I cross my leg at the knee. I'm wearing clean, black Nikes. I've never owned a pair of dress shoes or a tie in my life.

"We don't allow that kind of shoe," she says, pointing with the eraser end of her pencil. "To be honest with you, just that you'd wear those to an interview gives me concern."

"Sorry. I wasn't aware."

"And the hair," she says, gesturing with the pencil again. "I'd cut it if I were you. Some of our people get a little grabby. You don't want somebody getting a handful of your hair."

"I can handle grabby," I tell her. "I've worked with that before too."

"We'll let you slide for now," she says. "But be sure to study that guidebook before you begin."

"Begin?"

"You're hired," she says flatly, stacking my papers into a folder and sliding it into the larger of the two piles. "Everything's already been filed. Your start date is set for two weeks from this coming Wednesday. That should give you time to get your affairs in order elsewhere."

"Elsewhere?"

She turns her head to the side and gives me a look like her patience is fading fast. "To give notice at other jobs?" she says, the sound of her voice like a deflating balloon. "If you want to moonlight, that's up to you. But this is an extremely demanding position and if your work slacks even just a little, you won't last."

"Yes ma'am, thanks," I tell her. "I appreciate the chance."

"I'm going to shoot you straight about one thing more, Mr. Blaine. The only reason you got hired is because the agency is extremely understaffed right now," she says. "But keep your head down and do right and you should be fine."

"Head down, do right," I reply, standing and shaking her hand again. "Got it."

"And don't forget the guidebook," she adds. "You look it over real good. Not everyone here is as easygoing as me."

THIRTY-SEVEN

THANKS FOR THE PUSH

"For the creation was subjected to futility."

–ROMANS 8:20 NASB

THERE ARE TIMES IN LIFE WHEN YOU CAN SEE THE OFF-ramp coming. A place where you can pull off the highway and settle in. It's not a bad thing. Everybody dreams about finding their place, don't they? Where you fit? Where you can settle in? Where you can breathe all the way out and back in again?

It's not a bad thing, right?

I'M DRIVING TO CHURCH SUNDAY MORNING, REHEARSING my words. Brookie really is a great girl. Good-hearted, attractive. Every guy in church is after her. A good catch, they say. So when the service is over I'm going to take her to the Bok Bok Wok and tell her sorry I've been so distant lately but I've been thinking and maybe we should give it a try. You know. Something more than friends.

The other day I saw her walking across campus talking to this schlumpy girl with thick glasses and crooked teeth, and I could tell by the way Brookie was laughing and leaning in that she was truly being kind to this person who probably didn't have many friends. Not for Jesus points or because she knew someone was looking. Because it's just who Brookie is.

So right there watching the two of them walk along I remembered Terry's advice and prayed, *Okay, Jesus. Is this the right girl for me?*

Which one? Jesus replied.

Ah, Jesus. You so funny.

You can't live scared all your life. You have to try things to find out. Step out on faith. But is the chemistry there? I've got all this information about human behavior and relationships, but it's overwhelming still. Love is strange chemistry, good medicine when you get it right, volatile when it goes wrong. And the emotions of love and dysfunction can feel so much the same. What makes a relationship work? Man, I don't know.

I pull in and park in an open spot. Late for church again. Oh well. *Hail Mary, full of grace. Help me Jesus. Here goes.*

I fix my hair and clothes in the front glass. Dressed up today. Even borrowed loafers and a suit jacket from a friend. Taking a deep breath, I walk through the door. Brother Sammy catches my sleeve in the foyer. "Hey, Jamie," he says. "Where you been lately?"

"Just a bunch of stuff with work," I tell him. "And you know, things."

"Stuff and things," he nods, pulling at the lapels of his tangelo-colored sports coat. "Well, good to see you back. So what's the deal with you and Brooke?"

"Uh, why do you ask?"

"I saw her sitting with Brother Ernie this morning, the new music guy? I hear they've been spending a lot of time together."

"Yeah," I tell him. "Me and Brooke are just friends. Ernie's a good guy."

"So you knew?"

"Oh, sure," I lie. "She told me."

"Sorry, Jamie," Sammy says, wincing and bumping his fist against my arm. "Just didn't want you to find out when you went in."

"Really," I reply. "It's fine."

There's a squall of feedback and Sammy heads off toward the soundboard. I'm standing with one hand on the sanctuary door, waiting to enter, trying to figure out how I should feel. Sad? Mad? Conflicted? Let down?

Confused as ever before?

I turn and cut back through the foyer and out the front door. Across the lot to my cheap little rental car. The morning sun is blinding so I slip on my shades and crank the motor. And crank. And crank . . .

Great. Must have accidentally left the dome light on again. Man, I miss the Trooper. I'm just not used to this thing. I knock the gear into neutral and walk the car back into the street. I should be able to get up enough speed to pop the clutch and push start from here. The road is flat and it'll take a good long sprint. Hot today. So I tie my hair back and start pushing.

I don't know who gets dibs on serendipity. Maybe God and the devil trade it back and forth. Because just as I'm steadily huffing that Kia up the block and my fake Ray-Bans are slipping down my nose, I look over and half the church is staring at me out the side window. And what two faces are right there on the front end pew?

Of course.

I dig in double time and when I jump in to pop the clutch my loafer falls off in the street. I fire the engine, rev the Kia hard, and squeal tires down to the stop sign. Pull the parking brake. Limp back to get my shoe. Seems like a hundred-mile walk in the mean midday sun. I stoop down to grab it. The asphalt is burning. Most of the church has turned back but Brookie watches still. The gears of the universe pause. I wait, stooped in the road, staring back through the side church glass. And the look she gives me is pity.

Loafer in hand, I straggle back to the Kia and drive away.

Down Riverside. Through the gates and up the spiral stairs. Blanket over the rail. Cold and pitch-black room. I lie in the dark for the longest time, just thinking. But I don't want to think anymore. Just before sleep comes I pray.

Thanks, Jesus, I tell him. *Thanks for the push.*

THIRTY-EIGHT
PRETTY DANG SWEET

*"Unless you change and become
like little children, you will never
enter the kingdom of heaven."*

—MATTHEW 18:3 GW

A SIX-YEAR-OLD GIRL IN PIGTAILS AND PINK PANTS STANDS at the edge of the DJ booth, holding her pockets and twisting from side to side.

Nikki bumps my elbow. "That kid wants you," she says.

I wheel over and lean down. She's wearing tortoiseshell glasses with tape around the hinge and a Yosemite Sam Band-Aid across her left elbow. She is so tiny.

"Will . . ." She takes a nervous breath and looks back toward the picnic tables scattered through the snack bar. Her mother nods her on. "Will you come skate with me?" the little girl asks.

We all skate with the kids now and then but the rink is packed and the night is peaking fast. I really don't have time.

"Pleeease," she says.

I stand and look to the girl's mother. She's heavyset and tired around the eyes, in knit pants and a polyester blouse. Her hair is chopped in the style common to middle-school teachers and discount accountants working the fast-tax booth by the Walmart checkouts. Despite that, there's an air of cheerfulness about her as she nods that it's okay and gives a little shrug that says, *My kid's kind of a strange bird but what can you do?* Seems I've seen that look on someone's mother before.

Please? the mom mouths. The kid fidgets and chews her little finger, her face like a Chihuahua locked in the car.

"Go," says Nikki. "I'll DJ, you watch the floor."

I step over the chain and hold out my hand. The tiny girl takes it and we make our way out. She jerks her feet along, tipping forward and then back, clinging to my arm, *skritch skritch skrtich*ing in Fisher-Price kiddie skates, blue and yellow with the wheels locked.

"What's your name?" I ask.

"Dani," she says. "But Mama, she calls me Daffy."

"Which do you prefer?"

"Sir?"

"What name do you like best?"

She smiles. Her front teeth are missing and there's some strawberry Fun Dip spilled down her shirt. "I like Daffy," she says.

We shuffle along; she pulls at my hand. "What's your name?"

"My mama calls me Daffy too."

"Oh," she says, mulling it over, then gives me the side-eye. "Really?"

"Nah, I'm kidding," I tell her. "My name's Jamie James."

"I'm in first grade," she says, holding up a finger.

As we ease from the carpet to the hardwood floor, Nikki calls for couples only.

"Moooonlight couple skate," she says, covering the mic to giggle.

Thanks, Nik.

The other skaters straggle away leaving only two other pairs on the floor. Daffy pedals and totters, trying to keep up. She kicks off with her right foot, wobbles, then falls back. Stands, grabs at my fingers, and falls flat again. Over in the snack bar, Mama cranes her neck to see.

A teen couple slides by in graceful arcs. Daffy stares longingly as they pass then shifts her sad eyes to me. "I'm sorry," she says. "I can't skate too good."

I start to help her over to the carpet and back to her mom when Celine Dion and R. Kelly hit the epic chorus of "I'm Your Angel." Reaching down, I catch Daffy beneath the arms and lift her into the air. Her face freezes; she grips at the sleeves of my shirt.

"Are you scared?" I ask.

"N-No," she says, pointing to the couple. "I wanna skate like that."

"Then you better hold on," I tell her, as I sweep her up off the floor.

We dip and sway, lost in the sparkle and twirl, mirror balls throwing a thousand tiny shards of light, the music all around. Like gliding over glass, we weave beneath the disco glow and through the purple smoke. As I circle and swoop backward, she throws out her arms and soars.

Celine and Kelly's voices join together as one and Daffy sings along, about clouds up in the sky, faith and grace and angels, no matter who or where you are.

The teen couple cruises beside us; we figure eight and intertwine, mirroring each other's moves. Just before they drift away the teenage girl reaches out and touches Daffy's hand.

It's the kind of moment when time slows and every detail bleeds living color like Instamatic film, when your throat catches because for a brief few seconds life is as beautiful as you'd always hoped. When God shows up in the smile of a shy child and shows you something ten years of church Sundays couldn't contain. And when God arrives that way, there's something between laughing and crying, sweet as both at the same time, the notion that maybe, if that's what God is like, then things could be all right.

I pivot toward the middle of the floor, beneath the biggest mirror ball, spinning us round and round, becoming one with the blur of fog and lights and loud music. She closes her eyes, flutters her hands from side to side, and laughter bubbles forth like springs of pure joy.

Standing at the snack bar wall, her mother waves and claps her hands. "*Whoo*, Daffy!" she calls.

As the song ends, with one last spin, I set her gently at her mother's feet.

"Mama! Did you see, Mama?" Daffy says.

"I saw, baby," Mama answers. "What do you say?"

Daffy hugs me, tight as she can. "Thank you, Jamie James."

"Thank you," her mom seconds, pushing the hair from Daffy's face.

"No," I reply. "Thank you."

"Aw," Nikki sighs when I make it back to the booth. "Now how sweet was that?"

"Pretty dang sweet," I say.

THIRTY-NINE

BETTER THAN ZAXXON

"Every time I go to the ill, the dying,
the lonely, it becomes obvious after a
few moments that the only words that
matter are words of communion."

—EUGENE PETERSON

LACEY FROM THE CHURCH CHOIR PULLS ME TO THE SIDE
and asks if I'll go to the hospital to talk to her brother, who at age
forty-seven has decided to stop fighting cancer and die.

"He's refusing chemo this time," she says, "and he's got everybody all mad and sad and . . . just worried sick. Jerry Wayne, God
bless him, in a lot of ways is still just a big stubborn kid. He can
be a pain but we love him. And we're not ready to lose him yet."

She shows me his profile on the Internet, a sunburned red-
neck with a Porky Pig face, standing on the tailgate, holding a
stringer of bass in one hand and a Bud Light in the other. The
tag beneath his picture reads, "The Coolest Old SOB You'll
Ever Meet."

Lacey smoothes her eyebrow with her little finger and gives me an apologetic look. "We're not real sure where he is spiritually," she says. "He doesn't care much for preachers but I figure maybe he'll talk to somebody like you."

Sixth floor, room 640. There's the hissing of machines and IV drips, and the smell of disinfectants is like chemical death. Jerry is propped in a hospital bed watching LSU and Notre Dame on ESPN Classic, his face concave and gray now, hair cropped close.

"You the man here to talk me outta dyin'?" he asks with a grin.

"Nah," I tell him. "I'm here to meet that cool old SOB I read about on the Internet."

"You got him," he says with the firmest handshake he can manage. "Better hurry though. Offer expires soon."

"That's what I heard."

Jerry looks back as the eighties-era LSU boots it up for three. "Hundred thousand bucks to live what?" he says. "Six more months maybe? A year? Forget that. Ain't no quality life, either. Lacey can take that money and buy her kids some college."

I pull a chair up by his bed. "So what are you gonna do?"

"Leavin' it up to the Man, I guess," he says, looking to the sky. "See what's on the other side."

"What do you think is on the other side?"

Jerry fumbles with his IV and looks hard into my eyes. "I hope it's good," he says, with resonance. "And I hope they let me in."

"Good," I repeat. "What would *good* be?"

"You know, I been thinkin' about that." Jerry adjusts his pillow and places his hands behind his head. "You from the church, right?"

"Sort of," I reply. "But not really."

Jerry nods, satisfied with my nonanswer. "I went to church a lot when I was a kid. All that streets of gold and pearl gates—what's a gold street worth when you're dead?"

"Never understood that either."

Jerry mutes the TV and turns to face me. "My old man was tough and he loved his whiskey but he always made sure we didn't do without. Every Friday afternoon he'd slip me a ten-dollar bill and say: 'Boy, go spend it. Spend it like there ain't no tomorrow. You got the rest of your life to be careful.'"

"You were, what then?" I ask. "In high school?"

"Early high school, yeah. Mama'd drop me off at Godfather's Pizza, meet some friends. I'd eat about six pieces of black olive and ham, drink a pitcher of Dr. Pepper, and play the fire out of some *Zaxxon*." His eyes light up. "I remember the night I finally beat high score. Jukebox was playing "Rebel Yell" and Becky Brister kissed me by the bathrooms."

"I love *Zaxxon*," I tell him.

"You played *Zaxxon*? You ain't old enough to played no *Zaxxon*."

"Big-time. It's still around."

"Old memories," he says, shaking his head. "Young and free, your whole life ahead of you. Not a care in the world. What you wouldn't give to feel that way again. Flirtin' with girls and laughing with your buddies. Biggest problem I had was trying to beat that—what was at the end of *Zaxxon*?"

"Dragon."

"Dragon was *Super Zaxxon*," Jerry says with a snap of his fingers. "Regular *Zaxxon* had a robot. His arm shot missiles."

"Robot," I reply, mimicking its firing arm. "The Piggly Wiggly up close to my house had a *Super Zaxxon* near produce. It was cold in there all summer long. Used to hang out with a roll of quarters trying to kill that blasted dragon."

Jerry lets out a hoarse laugh and cuts his eyes. "You say you was a chaplain?"

"Naw."

"Lacey said you were some kind of counselor or something though, right?"

"Just some dude who used to play *Zaxxon*."

Jerry laughs again and shifts back over in the bed. When he adjusts the covers, I catch a glimpse of skin and bones, bruises from purple and black to sickly green, a jagged gash zippered with stitches near the low part of his back. He sees my shudder and says, "Hey brother, it's all right. I'm not in pain."

I nod for a while, not saying anything. The IV trickles down drip by drip as Jerry's pulse blips slowly across the screen.

"So what do you think's up there?" he asks, pointing up. "Gold streets is fine but . . . that ain't heaven for somebody like me."

"Jerry, I hope Jesus picks you up at the gate and takes you straight to Godfather's. There'll be old friends and all-you-can-eat pizza and endless pitchers of Dr. Pepper. Then he'll pull you to the side and say, 'Got a lil' surprise for you.' And he'll take you out past the moon to play real-life *Zaxxon*, with a spaceship and everything."

"Now that'd be some kinda cool right there," Jerry says.

"And instead of Billy Idol on the jukebox, he'll be there live," I tell him.

"If Billy Idol makes it, I guess we'll all be okay," he says.

"Ain't that the truth."

He lays back and stares at the ceiling; a calm look sweeps over his face. "Then maybe Jesus'll say, 'Hey Jerry. Your daddy's here.'"

I think about my own parents, the money they gave me for rock music and video games. I think about seeing them young again someday where everything's redeemed and nothing is lost again. I know Jerry is thinking the same thing because the room is heavy with that emotion. He pulls his hand across his eyes and smiles. "Dyin' man ain't ashamed to cry," he says.

"Hey, when you see your mom and dad again and they're young and ain't ever gonna get old," I say. "That's better than *Zaxxon*."

Jerry pulls himself closer by the rail of the bed. "You really believe that?" he asks.

Sometimes I wish I couldn't read people. It's a knowing born from one brief moment, a look paired with the tone of voice, the way their hands move with a question or certain words.

His knuckles are scarred from bar fights and working on old junk cars. There was a woman he loved and trusted and she broke his heart. I see him sitting alone a lot of long nights, drinking and wondering where life went wrong.

The echo of old hurts lingers in his eyes, disappointments and desperation, never really finding a place or a way to be all right. Maybe this is Jerry's way, his hope of finally finding his place to be all right.

"I really do," I tell him. "I believe Jesus meets us on the other side, just like we are. And he loves us. And he makes everything all right."

"Don't nobody really know for sure though, do they?" he says.

"Guess not," I reply. "But I believe what you hope is more important than what you know."

"I believe that too," he says, resting his fist on top of my hand. "Tell Lacey."

"She kinda needs to hear it from you."

Jerry pauses, looking past me. "All right."

LSU is first and goal, fourth quarter, late. When the ref throws his flag, Jerry coughs and says to me, "You ain't a preacher, huh?"

"Nah."

"You oughta be. You oughta go preach about Billy Idol and *Zaxxon* in heaven. Then maybe folks wouldn't be afraid to die."

"Kinda help with the living part, too, wouldn't it?" I tell him.

"Can I tell you a secret?" Jerry says.

"Yeah."

"Don't tell Lacey this part. Wait, okay?"

"Okay."

Jerry leans to me, his eyes clear. He waits and measures his words, making sure I catch each one. "I can't explain it. But I'm more at peace than I've ever been in my life."

You hear all kinds of things listening to people for a living. But every now and then there's something so different and true that it shakes you and makes you wonder how much of our lives are spent in the shallow end of the pool, so much unspoken and unknown. When someone trusts you with words like these, there's nothing to say in return. You receive it as a gift, like you've just caught a rare glimpse of the world that lies beneath the ocean.

All I can add is this: "That's rich, brother. Thank you."

We watch the Fighting Tigers flicker and score as the final seconds tick away. Purple and gold fill the screen. "It's still good even though you know who wins," Jerry says.

As the game ends, I stand to leave and wish him well.

"If I don't see you here again," he says with a grin. "I'll see you out past the moon."

FORTY

LET GO OF THE ROPES AND FADE AWAY

"Be anxious for nothing."

–JESUS

THE TWIN BRIDGES MALL IS DEAD EMPTY AT 8:25 ON A Tuesday night. Generally, I hate shopping malls. Except when they're dead empty and the store gates are halfway down, Muzak piping through long, wide halls of dark wood and white-pearl lights. You can walk and think and nobody pays you much mind.

I hate good-byes. Always have. That's why I haven't really told anybody about the state job thing. The timing never seems right, so I keep putting it off. I don't know. Guess I'd rather cut back gradually—leave a little at a time. That way it's not so hard. It's better just to fade away.

If I were Jesus I would have fixed life where you go from glory to glory, one great moment to the next, cradle-to-grave amazing and all the way back to heaven again. I would have fixed it where you could be a little more sure.

There's a tobacco shop called the Tinder Box at the dogleg in the mall. An armored knight guards the door, and when it's open the sweet smell of pipe smoke saturates the air. Just across the way there's a fountain where children and young lovers throw coins. So I stop, breathe sweet smoke, and throw three nickels into the stream. I'm not superstitious, but sometimes wishes come true.

Silence and trust. Secret places. Disappear and find the seams.

There's an announcement over the PA system urging me to make my final selections, that the mall will be closing soon. The Tinder Box manager steps out, pulls the knight inside, and shuts the door. I throw one last dime in the fountain and walk on.

It's a quarter till when I duck into Missy's Men's Fashions and Shoes. There's a big dude working the floor with a low-key Mohawk and tattoos sneaking from the cuffs of his button-down shirt. "Help you find something?" he asks, rattling the bullet bracelet around his wrist.

"Starting a new job tomorrow," I tell him. "Just need to grab some shoes and pants."

"No pressure," he says. "Let me know if I can help."

I pick out khakis, no pleat, and a pair of black lace-ups. Carry them to the counter. Never owned a pair of dress shoes before. "Cash or credit?" Mohawk Man asks.

I slide out the Discover Card I got from an offer addressed, "Hello, new graduate!" My name's embossed at the bottom and I run my fingers over it one letter at a time. Feels a little like a deal with the devil. Indulge now, suffer later. Never had a credit card before either. Change is necessary. Change is good. Change is a little scary sometimes.

"Credit," I reply.

He swipes the card and bags up my stuff. "These are nice shoes," he says. "I've got the same pair. You can work in them all day and they don't hurt your feet."

"You like this job?" I ask.

"It pays the bills," Mohawk replies, rattling his bracelet again.

"Pays the bills," I repeat.

"You do what you got to, Cowboy," he says. "Find a way to make it your own. I can be whoever I want to be once I walk out that back door."

I figure the assistant manager at Missy's Men's Fashions is as good a source of wisdom as any. "How do you know who you want to be?"

"Guess that's the tricky part," says Mohawk, hand on his chin, cracking his neck. "But if it was easy, everybody'd have it figured out."

Back at home, I lay out the new shoes and khakis with the button-down polo I got at the Goodwill off St. Paul. As long as I roll the sleeves up, the ink stain doesn't show. "You can't wear white socks with khakis and dress shoes," Mohawk told me.

"What do you mean, I can't?"

"Well," he said, slipping a pair of black socks into the bag. "You shouldn't."

I've got the whole uniform on a chair by the bed. I step back and give it a look. It's late for the real world but I'm still restless. So I make my way through the grotto to the hedge maze out back. There's only one path to the center but I like to walk them all. After wandering each row, I pick the right one and take it to the middle where a statue of Mother Mary resides.

"Ma'am," I ask reverently, if not a little desperately, "what's the secret of life?"

The Lady stands graceful, silent as stone, the smallest hint of a smile on her lips. I climb the marble base and stand beside her, looking out over the estate. Rest my head against her awhile.

"I hear ya, Mama," I reply.

With thanks to the Lady, I hop down and walk to the mailbox at the end of the drive. Junk mail. Bill. Postcard from the dentist reminding me I'm overdue to get my teeth cleaned. *Classic Rock* magazine. An official-looking letter sits last in the pile. I head back to the house, climb the stairs, and tear the seal. Sit next to the bed and look it over for a long time.

It's still early for me. My bike is parked in the gazebo by the pool. I slip it out and coast down Sweet Olive Lane. The street is cool and shaded. Floodlights are strung sparsely through the tops of the tallest pines. The charcoal Aussie darts from her side yard and meets me at the corner of Jasmine, pacing alongside until she stops before the long curve, watching as I pedal away. Beyond the dead-end sign there's a narrow path that rises over the levee and into the trees. Where the thicket breaks there's a trail leading to a cove hidden by the riverside.

I sit on the bank, staring into black waters while stars fall and the calling song of cicadas surrounds me. A slim tower spirals high above the tree line, red lights blinking softly down its side, the needle tip vanishing into the clouds.

> *In returning and rest, you will be saved.*
> *In silence and trust you will find your strength.*

A slow barge drifts across the river on the far side, its wake rolling toward the shore. Sometimes you need a marker where the old life ends and new begins. So I wade into the water to meet the wake. Knee deep first and then to the waist. The river is warm against me as the water rises to my chest. Just before the current hits, I lean back, catch a long last breath, and let the dark waters take me down.

IT'S 6:15 A.M. I POUR A BOWL OF COCOA PEBBLES AND scan through a passage from Matthew while I eat. Today's devotion: *Let go of the ropes*, says Jesus. *Live light and free. Learn to walk in the unforced rhythms of grace.* I flip to the front and read the inscription again. *Jamie baby, just be you.*

I shave, tie my hair back, and pull the stiff khakis on. Thrift-store polo tucked, new shoes laced up tight. The sun is bright and traffic thick as I make my way across town to a windowless federal building, third floor.

"On time is late," the supervisor informs me. "And fifteen minutes early is on time." There's one clear spot on her desk. I lay the paper there. "What's this?" she growls.

Always count five seconds in your mind before any serious reply. A rough-cut old riverboat gambler from rehab taught me that. *Thousand one, thousand two . . .*

"Resignation," I tell her. "I appreciate the chance but something better came along. Just wanted to come down and tell you face-to-face."

She looks the paper over and grunts back. "Didn't figure you'd last."

"Yes ma'am," I reply, laying down her guidebook too. "You figured right."

I beep the Kia's horn all the way back across town and wave at the nannies pushing strollers down the walk. Around the bend and up the spiral stairs. A blanket hangs over the rail to block out the sun. I lay still for the longest time, staring at the lights as they sparkle and dim. The endless surf rolls through a cold dark room. There's a slip in time just before sleep comes when all that will ever be is well. *Thanks be to God.* Peace like a river till I fade away.

FORTY-ONE

777: FAVOR

"Follow peace."

–HEBREWS 12:14 KJV

IT'S 9:20 ON A WEDNESDAY NIGHT. THERE'S A PAIR OF OLD scissors in the kitchen drawer. Sometimes you need to do something foolish just to feel sane again. So I cut the khakis a few inches above my knee. Rat out a loose strip, tie it around my head and tease my hair up high. Cut that credit card, too, while I'm in the mood. Jump on my bike and pedal toward the Quik Stop up the way.

It's a warm night but the breeze off the water is cool. The moon is veiled but now and then the crescent sneaks through and makes the clouds around it shine silvery grey. I ride through silent streets, searching dark windows, wondering if I'm the only fool out watching the moon.

Thanks for the moon, I tell God. *I appreciate it—I really do.* I wonder if I'm the only fool who ever thanks God for the moon.

I lean my bike against the Quik Stop wall and head inside. Eazy Stevie the cashier is leaning over the counter, twisting her hair with one finger while reading the local style magazine. She glances up and gives me a quick "Hey."

"Hey girl," I reply.

She spins the magazine round to me. "You think my hair'd look good like this?" There's a picture of a dancer with dirty blond hair, shaved in the back and long down front with red frosted tips.

"Sure," I say. "Why not?"

"Really?" she says. "I'm kinda scared to cut it."

"It's hair," I tell her, pulling mine over my eyes. "It'll grow back."

"Yeah," says Stevie. "Guess you're right."

I drag the magazine closer. There's a photo next page over of a pale ballerina in an Aerosmith shirt. "That one," I tell Stevie, tapping the page. "Her."

"What about her?"

"I don't know. Somethin'," I reply, tossing a dollar onto the counter. "Hey, can I get four quarters?" I dig out another three bucks and slide the money her way. "Peach ICEE and a Diet Coke."

"We're out of peach," she says. "Wild cherry all right?"

"Wild cherry's just fine."

"Help yourself, then," Stevie says, punching register buttons and pointing toward the back.

When she gives me the change I notice three sevens written with a Sharpie on the palm of her hand. "What's that mean?"

"This?" she says, turning her wrist. "I was flipping channels last night and some preacher said 777 was the number of perfection. Then he started talking about favor and how God had my name written on his hands. Been a tough few months, man. Figured I need all the favor I can get."

"Heard that," I tell her, reaching palm up. "Write it on my hand too."

She pulls out a pen and draws three sevens in the middle of my hand. "Here ya go," she says. "Right across your Heart line."

"Oh yeah," I reply. "Cool."

"Yep," she nods. "Cool." Stevie smacks her gum and leans back over the magazine, one finger twisting her hair.

They swapped out *Black Knight* a while back and now *Twilight Zone* pinball sits in its place next to the ICEE machine. I plug in my money and the table pops to life, neon flashing, bumpers thumping as the theme song begins, a solid white Powerball waiting in the lane. The best thing about pinball is there's no room to think about anything but now.

I launch the ball across the field and through the ramps, slingshot rockets and slot machines, magna-flip pyramids and super-skill shots, gunning for high score. A pair of customers approaches from the far right side, just out of my sight line.

"Well, hello there, Jamie."

I cradle the ball on the flipper and turn. "Hello, Sister Brooke," I reply.

Ernie tucks the milk and bread beneath his arm and firmly shakes my hand. "What are you doing here?" she asks.

I catch our reflections in the beer cave door. Brooke and Brother Ernie look like Ken and Barbie in their Wednesday church best. I'm in hacked-off khakis and a ratty old Sabbath tee with the neck and sleeves cut out, makeshift bandana tied up under my hair, leaning over a pinball machine sucking on a wild cherry ICEE. What I should tell her is that I'm walking in the unforced rhythms of grace and living light and free. I'm not really that quick on my feet though.

"Uh, nothin'," I reply. "Just hangin' out."

"You okay, brother?" Ernie asks. "We heard about your wreck. Been praying for you ever since."

"Thanks, man. Keep praying. I'll take all I can get."

"How's your head?" says Brooke.

"It's fine," I tell her, pulling the bandana loose. "Wanna see the scar?"

She reaches up and touches over my ear. "Ew," she says. "It's like a big dent."

"No, that's an old one." I laugh. "Feel lower down."

"Heard you took a job with the state?" she says, wincing as she runs her finger over the spot where the stitches came out.

"You heard right," I reply. "Today was my first day."

"How do you like it?"

"Today was my last day too," I say. "Wanna hear a good story?"

"One of your rambling stories?"

"More like a testimony. I'll make it short. Came home last night, bootstraps and big-girl panties, ready to give it my best. Just before bed I check the mail. Letter from the insurance company. Not mine—the lady's who hit me. Finally admitting it was her fault. One check for my truck, three thousand more than I paid for her. Even bigger check for getting hit in the head. I stayed up till four, drove over this morning, and quit."

"That's a tough way to make some money, Jamie."

"Really? I thought it was pretty easy. My plan is to just keep getting hit in the head every six months or so."

Brooke and Ernie look back and forth, somewhere between confusion and concern.

"Nah, I'm kidding. I called the insurance guy and told him I didn't need some big head-injury check. Cover the bills and I'm fine. But they insisted on something so we worked out a deal. You know though, it got me to thinking. How much money do I really need to be happy and get by? I can live on less. It's like, there's all this pressure to get your life figured out and together, but I don't believe that's the most important thing. Ambition's overrated. Things have a way of working out, y'know?"

"Okay, you're starting to ramble," Brooke says, covering her face not to laugh. "So what are you going to do now?"

"DJ at the roller rink. Crisis at night. Little at the counseling center now and then."

"That's the plan?"

"For now," I tell her. "I think I'm where I'm supposed to be."

I smile and she smiles and Brother Ernie slides his hands into his pockets and rocks back on his heels. I've got the Powerball trapped on the right flipper, waiting. "Well," I tell her, "good seeing y'all."

"Same here," she says. "You are still in church though, right?"

"I'm in church right now." Every once in a while I think of a good reply. Brooke hugs me from the side as Brother Ernie shakes my hand.

"Take care, Jamie James," she says.

"You too, Brookie Brooke." They pay, walk out, and climb into his Civic. We exchange a last wave before they drive away.

The Powerball is ceramic, much lighter than steel. SHOOT LEFT LOOP FOR MULTIBALL . . . the LEDs scroll. I fire the ball and nail the loop. The bumpers blaze as the table explodes in a cacophony of light and pinballs fall from every angle. Eyes flittering, I try to follow, slinging them through the ramps into super-skill shots, jackpots, blast-off rockets, again and again until one by one they slip away. Only one remains as I chase the high score through the right ramp and around the left, into the pyramid, magna-flip, nudge and bump the table with my hip . . . TILT. Last ball down the drain.

I step back with hands to the side of my head and take a long breath.

ENTER YOUR INITIALS . . . the LEDs scroll . . . NUMBER 2!

The Quik Stop is eerie quiet now. High score stands. I can't help but drop my hands and laugh as the initials KKX flash over mine. The ICEE cup is nearly empty so I crack the Diet Coke and fill it back to the brim. I've got four more ones wadded in my pocket and the store is open all night.

"Hey," Stevie calls. "Who was that chick?"

"Just a friend," I reply.

There's a radio on a shelf behind the register and the DJ plays a song about living after midnight till the dawn. Stevie reaches over and turns it loud.

"777," I shout, lifting my hand.

"Favor!" She salutes, holding up her own.

FORTY-TWO

WHEREVER YOU ARE TONIGHT

"Now faith is the substance of things hoped for."

—HEBREWS 11:1 KJV

SUNDAY NIGHT CHURCH. I'M SITTING IN THE BALCONY, looking over the people as they sing. Voices twine together, rising to the highest beam, in a song about when things feel hopeless and dreams lay shattered on the ground, when the path seems dark and it's just so hard to find a way to keep moving on.

There's a fellow in the second row fighting suicide and a divorced woman on the platform who's running out of excuses for the reasons that she needs all those pills. There's a couple near the back who've been asked to leave three churches now. The man on center aisle with shaking hands. Singers struggling to stay in the closet, preachers living secret lives. Some here are so depressed and anxious that it's a major victory even to make it through the door.

But here we are.

Look up, the people sing. *It's not over. You can find a way to start again.*

We are all such wrecks down here. Strangers in a strange land, falling time and time again. Trying to find a way to live right and love each other without losing our minds. Pretending and doing the best we can. Spinning our wheels and holding on to life as it slowly slips away.

But there's something truly beautiful about wrecked people standing together and singing about grace and ways to make it through. Hoping still, even as the light fades and good dreams die, even when the way seems lost, even as kingdoms fall, even through the long, dark night of quiet skies.

Save us, Oh God, for the waters rise.

Here we are on this blue speck floating through the endless night, spiraling across a measureless cosmos of chaos and majesty, searching, reaching, longing for something higher than ourselves.

Here we are in this one small room, together, separate, united, alone. Our worst so rotten and our best so good. Struggling, trying, falling, failing. Rising from the dust and returning again. Believing for something better—something more.

Here we are, God, the wreck of your hands, fashioned from dirt and breath, blood and water, spirit and flesh, beauty and chaos. Strangers unaware, hoping for something beyond the endless night.

The hope that an infinite Creator rose up through this same dust and walked our planet as a man, tempted and tried, falling and rising again—the hope that someday we will rise up and never fall again—that's what holds us all together. Searching for the weight, the counterbalance, the antidote to this one strange tiny life. Searching for ways to hold on and keep hope alive.

As long as there is hope.

The praise band fades away and we sing an old hymn about the friendship of Jesus while they pass the plate for a family who lost their home to a fire. I spot them near the middle, the father gripping the pew back and trying to stay strong, two teenage children leaning against the mother from opposite sides as she holds them tight, all of them crying, all singing now.

The sanctuary is still. We make another round through the chorus when the song leader circles with his hand. One woman rises from the back and rushes to the mother, wrapping arms around her. Across the sanctuary, people leave their seats and join in.

Attendance is thin in the balcony but a rumpled fellow with nightshift eyes walks over and passes me a silver plate. I sit staring, turning it in my hand. The sides are tarnished and the bottom red felt. There's a smattering of bills and offering envelopes stacked inside. I've been carrying around a cut of that insurance check, not sure why. I think I know now. I slide it into the plate and make my way down.

It's a little uncomfortable standing and waiting in the crowd. But I stick it out until there's a break, reach over, and touch the mother's arm. "Hey," I tell her, "if there's anything I can do."

"Thank you, baby," she says, squeezing my hand. She smiles through tears and pulls the younger teen close. "We just might take you up on that."

I nod and step away so others can press in. The preacher walks to the platform and stands with the microphone, quiet for a time. "I uh, realize this is out of order," he finally says. "But would you mind if first, we pray?"

Everyone turns to face the altar now. The piano player returns and plays the hymn softly once more.

"Bow your heads with me, please," the preacher says. "Eyes closed and hands stretched forth." There's a long pause before he speaks again. "All across this room, people are hurting. Some have lost homes. Others, family. Some feel as if they've lost themselves. But one thing's for sure; everyone here is struggling and trying to find their way. So let's just pray humbly, best we can. And I want to believe that God will meet you, wherever you are tonight."

I am so far from where I need to be. Still fumbling and bumping into walls. Sometimes it feels like I won't ever get it right. But I believe the message of Jesus is this: "I'm with you. Even to the end. Even if you never find some grand purpose or plan, even when you run into the walls again and again. Even if you fumble from the cradle to the grave. Even if you never get it right. I am with you. Even to the end."

I know I'm not supposed to, but instead of lowering my head I look up to the highest beam as the prayers rise around me. And for just one moment, there is the sweetest peace.

With every head bowed and every eye closed, I slip out the side door into the night.

Sunday, the hour before dusk. The first stars are rising and the moon is full. Doorbell lights down a dark street. The shepherd paces with me, sniffing the air. There's a place before the long curve where the oak trees gather at the shoulder, stretching heavy arms across the road. I pedal and coast through the shadows. The mansions are dim and streets bare. A slow wind sweeps up from the face of the waters. I close my eyes and stretch out my hands.

FORTY-THREE

JUST KEEP WALKING

"May he rule from sea to sea and from
the River to the ends of the earth."

–PSALM 72:8 NIV

IT'S 6:15 ON A FRIDAY NIGHT AND I'M DRIVING TO WORK AT the roller rink, taking the back way along the river's edge. There's a crossing just past the bend on Summer Lane where the road rises and the sun sets over the water, casting shimmers of gold across the way.

Bought another Trooper. Two years newer, silver with smoke-black tint. The rims don't rattle but I still try not to go over thirty-five. Just in case.

I paid off some of those student loans with the insurance money and the rest consolidated at a low rate. The church put me on payroll, just to do my thing—meet people wherever they are. It's only a few hours a week but that's all I really need. I don't even have an office anymore. Life's not that complicated. It doesn't take much to be all right.

Sometimes you need a ceremony to mark when seasons change. So I throw the truck in neutral and let her coast. Climb out and walk alongside, one hand holding the door.

There are a few fortune cookies scattered across the console and an empty ICEE cup with a Diet Coke bottle inside. Jonah's felt-board whale still waits in the wayback. Just couldn't bring myself to throw it away. An archaeological study Bible sits on the backseat next to a textbook on the history of classic rock. Roller Rabbit's picture is propped by the speedometer. Cousin It bobblehead on the dash. Thank you, radical Jesus, for radical hope and never-ending grace. For misfit wonder and ridiculous things. For riding shotgun with me through this strange and beautiful life.

The sun bleeds red like a mirage on the waters, shimmering all the way to where I stand. Everything is perspective, so it seems. One thing ends and another begins. Every frame of living like a photograph—everything now.

A VW Bug pulls up behind me, top down, and with AOII plates. Two brunettes toot their horn, waving as they pass. I wave back and climb inside the Trooper, driving a little faster now.

I take a left on the highway, into the Skate City lot. There's a line out front all the way down the walk and a gaggle of rink rats wait clustered and restless at the door. I slip in through the back and cue up my first few songs. Charge the smoke machines, enjoy the silence awhile.

"Are you ready?" asks Mr. Ric.

Lights pulse through the fog, and the music is loud. I flip the lock, open the doors wide, and laughing children rush around me.

"Ready," I reply.

THE SOUND OF THE RINK STILL RINGS IN MY EARS AS I TURN down Magnolia and pedal toward Sweet Olive Lane. I think I could ride this old bike forever. Down this dark ribbon until the lights from that city lead me home.

I coast through the shadows before the long curve. The shepherd rushes out from the side yard, her coat the color of the night. She paces with me fifty yards or so before pulling back. Instead of pedaling away, I swing around and ride circles in the street. She barks once, romping—darting ahead and behind me now.

I break from the circle and drive on. She sits in the middle of the street. I hit the brakes and slide sideways to a stop, one foot on the pedal and the other on the road. The shepherd cocks her head, that one white stripe shining behind her eyes, and we watch each other for the longest time.

Finally, she stands and walks to where I wait, sniffing around me, watching again. And when I ride she runs beside me, through the long curve and dashing into the sprinklers at the end of the lane. Past the dead-end sign and up the narrow path, across the levee to the other side. There's a break in the thicket where we cut down the bank to a hidden cove that sits just over the river's bend. If you sit still long enough your eyes adjust to the night and the stars shine that much brighter.

The Big Dipper points to the North Star. Falling stars aren't really stars at all. The light from the faintest twinkle traveled over a billion years to appear here tonight. Astronomy is the glory of the great unknown, enigma of all ages, the endless, nameless face of God.

Come away to a quiet place and I will give you rest
treasures of darkness in the secret place.

I lie back flat in the grass and stare into the infinite night. Hours pass like no time at all. Venus rises bright and blue. The shepherd wanders to where I lay. "I'll get it together," I tell her, scratching that one white stripe. "One of these days."

Stars on the water as the sweet old world turns slow, and God seems closer than your oldest, truest friend. All the reasons why don't matter anymore. Sometimes it's enough to just be still and breathe.

It's nearly midnight when the crisis line rings.

"Hello?"

Before the words, a long deep sigh. "I just really need to know someone else is out there tonight."

"Yeah," I tell the caller. "I'm here."

AFTER THE CREDITS ROLL

"Nothing ever really ends, does it?"

–CHUCK SHURLEY

HEY, THE BOOK'S OVER. WHAT ARE YOU STILL DOING HERE? Oh. You're wondering what happened to all those characters? Yeah, well, me too. Truth is, with most cases, I never get to know the end of the story. In church work and crisis psych you live with whatever closure you get.

That being said, I love the little section in a movie after the credits roll that tells the story after the story ends. It's casual. Fun but not pertinent. So in the spirit of epilogues, here are a last few scattered words—the best bit of resolution I can give.

THE PSYCH WARD PASTOR, BROTHER PONDER, PASSED AWAY. He left a good legacy. I bet Jesus said, "Come on in, my man. You did real good."

OL' BLUE died too. I went to his funeral because I figured there might not be many people showing up. I was wrong. It was packed. We told stories and sang "Amazing Grace." As funerals go, it was really fine.

I saw CHRIS, my grandmother's neighbor, at the Tractor Supply last June. He told me he was still clean and sober. "One day at a time, ever since that crazy night."

DIEGO works at the tire store off Ninth Street. He's a deacon now for the Spanish service.

BROTHER JOHN checked himself out of rehab and went back on tour. Then he relapsed again. Then he laid his whiskey bottle on the altar one Sunday night. I was dubious, but from what I hear, he's doing okay. Sometimes he picks up Brother Ponder's spot at the psych ward.

JACKIE the psych nurse died on the table during her second open-heart surgery. But they shocked her back to life. She told me she had a vision of the universe with a great light shining through from the other side. Then she saw a vase with a crack down the center and water leaking out. The voice of Jesus boomed from outer space.

"You are a badly broken vessel," he said. "But that's what I use to get the work done. So I'm sending you back. And when you're finished I'll bring you home with me forever."

She returned to the psych ward shortly thereafter, scarred from stem to stern, cigarette in one hand, oxygen tank in the other, a cracked pot spilling water everywhere she went.

HEATHER/SOFTBALL got her master's in counseling. I was her internship supervisor. Soon as she graduated, I offered her a job at the rink.

I brought my guitar and stopped by LARRY's a while back.

Even learned "By-Tor and the Snow Dog" so we could play it together. I wanted to tell Larry that our story made its way to the legendary Neil Peart and that he'd sent a very kind message saying it was a lot of fun, and how much he enjoyed reading it. Figured Larry would get a kick out of that. But the trailer was gone and only a rectangle of dead grass remained. Another life lesson. I'm sorry I waited too long.

One dark and cloudless night, JOHNNY RAY stepped in front of the train. Part of me was brokenhearted. Another part hoped he was finally home and free.

LIZA got herself straightened out and returned to work at the psych ward. She goes home at five sharp now, never works weekends, and is a much better counselor for it.

DR. CRYER now lives a farmer's life. "People are hard," he told me. "Cows are easy."

TERRY the psych ward night tech moved back to Indiana and was going to school to be a psych nurse.

GARRETT THOMAS is a ranger in the Smoky Mountains now. In his dreams. He's still a church counselor, trying to help Christians find their balance.

I never saw SUNSHINE again. But last I heard, KATY was telling her story here and there, helping other girls get straight.

KATHERINE/TAT married a contractor and moved to Beverly Hills. Florida, that is. Someone told me she has an autistic daughter and is a totally happy stay-at-home mom now.

Last summer, I stopped at the Quik Stop for a Diet Coke, when a familiar-looking fellow walked up and opened the next cooler down. He was wearing a yellow tank top with tan lines marked around the meaty part of his arms. His face was round, pink, and Piggly.

Can't be.

My memory doesn't always work well, so I held my tongue. He turned, reached out, and grabbed me by the shoulder. *"Zaxxon* preacher man!"

"JERRY?!" I was so bewildered all I could manage was, "You're still alive?"

"Yeah man, yeah," he laughed.

"Thought the next time I'd see you'd be out past the moon."

"Guess the Man had other plans," Jerry said with a laid-back grin.

"But—how?"

"It's a mystery," he said, stepping closer. "Doc sent me home, said there wasn't nothing else they could do. But my old granny said there wasn't no way I was goin' in the ground before she did. So I kept fishin' and Granny prayed." He stepped back and held out his arms. "And here I am."

"Whoa," I said. "So you're all right now?"

"I am today, brother," Jerry said. "And today's all we've got anyway."

Me and MOHAWK MAN from Missy's Fashions became good friends. Life is strange that way.

Never did beat KKX's high score. Not yet.

MR. RIC and the RINK roll on. If you pass through on a Friday night, you'll find disco balls and cotton candy, the happy sound of children laughing. And if you see ROLLER RABBIT? Be sure to get a picture and a hug. You just never know.

BROOKIE and BROTHER ERNIE got married. I sang at their wedding. "Freebird." Just kidding.

She got her MBA and now blogs obsessively about coffee

and her children. She and Brother Ernie did make some really cute kids.

I got a note from her a while back that said, among other things, "Sorry, I didn't handle things as well as I should have."

"No worries," I wrote back. "It all worked out for the best."

I married THE BALLERINA. But that's a story for another day.

———

GOD still walks in the cool dark night at the far end of Sweet Olive Lane.

Sometimes I hear him laugh.

GRATITUDE

WRITING A BOOK IS A LITTLE LIKE A MONKEY TRYING TO carve a bowling ball out of a mountain with a butter knife. So it helps to have an army of monkeys.

Super-agent Bryan Norman steers me right and saves me from the baby wasps. Nothing without you, Chico. And those nice people at Alive Literary Agency too.

A mighty fine editor and friend, Sister Texas, Debbie Wickwire. Kristi Smith, Lori Cloud, Nicole Pavlas, Adria Haley, Joel Kneedler, Matt Baugher, and all the staff of W Books/ Thomas Nelson in beautiful downtown Donelson, Tennessee.

Ms. Laura Weldon. Neely Baugh. Nate Anderson. Dr. Dana Carpenter. Michael Holmes and David Caron. The Outlaw Josie Renwah, Lee "Bodi" Swartz, Marc Byrd, and Andrew Thompson. Sean Beaudoin. Brother Joe Daly. Irene Zion. For those gracious early readers: Vicky Von Rotten—true follower of the misfit Jesus. Brothers Joshua Shenk and Josh Axelrad, who waded out to meet me in the muddy waters. Bev Mansfield and River Jordan, there from the start. For my so young parents who tried their best, took me to libraries, and taught me to be fiercely independent.

Every writer needs a patient spouse. Thank God for mine whose sweetness teaches me grace and peace, daily.

חבשה לאל

NOTES

AUTHOR'S NOTE

The image of "Peter cursing and falling beneath the waves" refers to Matthew 14:22–33, when Jesus walks out on the water to meet the disciples' boat.

- "Noah fed up and drunk" refers to Genesis 9:21: "Noah drank some wine, got drunk, and lay down naked right in the middle of his tent."

- "Thomas doubting" refers to John 20:24–29, when he asks Jesus for proof that he's really returned and risen from the dead.

- "David tiptoeing to get a second peek" refers to his spying on Bathsheba's rooftop bath in 2 Samuel 11:2–5.

- The story of "Jonah at midnight in the belly of the whale" can be found in Jonah 1–2.

- "Elisha calling down bears" refers to the time Elisha caused a bunch of angry bears to maul some kids who had been taunting him in 2 Kings 2:23–25.

JUST START WALKING
freewheeling roller rink DJ gets job offer at a mental hospital

· "Don't try to figure out everything on your own."
—Proverbs 3:5 THE MESSAGE

· "For we walk by faith, not by sight."—2 Corinthians 5:7 ESV

· "Teach us to number our days, that we may gain a heart of wisdom."—Psalm 90:12 NIV

· "The wild animals honor me, the jackals and the owls, because I provide water in the wilderness and streams in the wasteland, to give drink to my people, my chosen."
—Isaiah 43:20 NIV

· You can find an interview where I discuss the openly Christian message of early Sabbath songs with bassist/lyricist Geezer Butler—and another where former vocalist Glenn Hughes talks about beating the devil by the grace of God—at jamieblaine.com.

THIS IS NOT TV
in which a giant psychotic patient threatens to hit me with a chair

· "Be patient in tribulation, constant in prayer."—Romans 12:12 ESV

· "For God has not given us a spirit of fear and timidity, but of power, love, and self-discipline."—2 Timothy 1:7 NLT

· "I will . . . transform the Valley of Trouble into a gateway of hope."—Hosea 2:15 NLT

· The song nurse Jackie sings in the med room is "Seven Spanish Angels" by Ray Charles and Willie Nelson.

THERE BUT FOR THE GRACE

pyromaniacs and nympho schizophrenics in my first few weeks working the psych ward

- "So the LORD was sorry he had ever made them and put them on the earth. It broke his heart."—Genesis 6:6 NLT
- The scripture the priest read was Isaiah 30:15: "In returning and rest, you will be saved. In quietness and trust you will find strength" (THE VOICE).
- Country bands often put their own spin on R&B classics to keep the people dancing.

MONK BY DEFAULT

naïve psych major struggles to find the balance between faith and responsibility

- "If a certain quantity of gas is pumped into an empty chamber, it will fill the chamber completely and evenly, no matter how big the chamber. Thus suffering completely fills the human soul and conscious mind, no matter whether the suffering is great or little."—Viktor Frankl
- "Smoke. Nothing but smoke."—Ecclesiastes 1:2 THE MESSAGE
- "Humans are too temporal and moody to delay gratification. We are terrible at waiting and obsessed with reward. But if we weren't hardwired this way, we'd likely still be huddled in caves, not particularly concerned whether someone discovered fire or found better sources of food."—Dr. Stephens

- The "store up your treasures in heaven" plan in the Bible is discussed in Matthew 6:20: "But lay up for yourselves treasures in heaven, where neither moth nor rust destroys and where thieves do not break in and steal" (ESV).

- Proverbs 25:2 reminds us that it's the glory of God to conceal a matter, but the honor of kings to seek it out.

GOTTA RUN TO KEEP FROM HIDING
a familiar face on my first crisis call

- "Even though I am free of the demands and expectations of everyone, I have voluntarily become a servant . . . to reach a wide range of people: religious, nonreligious, meticulous moralists, loose-living immoralists, the defeated, the demoralized—whoever. I didn't take on their way of life . . . but I entered their world and tried to experience things from their point of view."
  —1 Corinthians 9:20–23 THE MESSAGE

OCEANS OF GRACE
where the psych ward pastor has his biggest altar call

- When Brother Ponder says, "Remember when he was trying to preach and that guy kept hollering out, 'Have mercy!'" he is referring to Mark 10:48.

- Mary Magdalene "barged in on the board meeting" in Luke 7:37.

- The "boys cut a hole in the roof during church so they could lower their sick buddy down" in Luke 5:19.

- Aftershave, shoe polish, and hair spray are frequent alternatives for desperate alcoholics.

- "I'm after mercy, not religion. I'm here to invite outsiders, not coddle insiders."—Matthew 9:13 THE MESSAGE

- "Make sure no one misses God's grace."—Hebrews 12:15 CEB

RAMBLE ON, OL' BLUE
in which a loveable old drunk teaches me a thing or two about the nature of God

- The part in the Bible Ol' Blue was referring to when he spoke of Jesus not always being so sure was likely when Christ quoted Psalm 22:1 in Mark 15:34.

- "Grace is all you need. My power works best in weakness."—2 Corinthians 12:9 NLT

- Insisting on a safe Bible and well-behaved Jesus neuters the grace of God.

THE GOLDEN TICKETS OF GOD
where I try to raise money for grad school by singing at a campus nightspot

- "If I have to boast, I will boast of what pertains to my weakness."—2 Corinthians 11:30 NASB

- "The Pharisees and the religion scholars were not all pleased. They growled, 'He takes in sinners and eats meals with them, treating them like old friends.'"—Luke 15:2 THE MESSAGE

- There are no reported stories of Jesus turning over tables in a bar.

GOLDEN TICKETS II, THE FIRST CLUE

we play a rocking Pentecostal revival and Jesus comes through last minute with the cash

- "Suddenly, there was a sound from heaven like the roaring of a mighty windstorm, and it filled the house where they were sitting."—Acts 2:2 NLT

- "Go to the lake and throw out your line. Take the first fish you catch; open its mouth and you will find a . . . coin." —Matthew 17:27 NIV

- The passage describing "blood red moons and crashing stars, [waiting] for lightning to split the eastern sky and rapture us over the jasper wall" refers to the events described when the world ends in Revelation. Revelation 21:18 describes heaven: "The wall was made of jasper, and the city of pure gold, as pure as glass."

- The part in the Bible where Jesus says, "Give no thought to tomorrow," is Matthew 6:34.

INTO THE VENT

where I climb into a wall to talk down a heartbroken office worker

- "A crushed reed he will not break, and a fading candle he won't snuff out."—Isaiah 42:3 ISV

- "The only true currency in this bankrupt world is what you share with someone else when you're not trying to be cool."—Lester Bangs

- Crawl spaces for storage are apparently common in older buildings.

LIFE IS CRAZY / AMAZING GRACE
testimony night at church proves a good place to study behavioral psychology

- "Are you tired? Worn out? Burned out on religion?" —Matthew 11:28 THE MESSAGE
- "Stop your silly efforts to save yourselves."—Isaiah 30:15 THE MESSAGE
- Brother Doobie's disco pants were shiny black cords with big front pockets and mammoth flares.

BROTHER JOHN AND THE RAGGED STRAGGLERS BAND
in which the police bring an evangelist to rehab

- "So the last shall be first, and the first last."—Matthew 20:16 NASB
- Individuals who are attracted to the emotionally intense elements of the Charismatic experience are also often drawn to behaviors such as substance abuse, sexual acting out, and criminal misconduct.
- Jesus said, essentially, "I didn't come for the religious people; I came for the misfits," in Matthew 9:13, Luke 5:32, and Mark 2:17. ("On hearing this, Jesus said to them, 'It is not the healthy who need a doctor, but the sick. I have not come to call the righteous, but sinners.'")
- Fellow Nashvillian Brandon Kinney wrote a great song about how, thank God, Jesus still runs with a rough crowd.

IN YOUR DREAMS
where I ponder life's meaning while roller skating through the grocery store

- Proverbs 18:24 speaks of the friendship of Jesus. "A man of many companions may come to ruin, but there is a friend who sticks closer than a brother."
- "Night is coming, when no one can work."—John 9:4 NIV
- Roller rinks have an exclusive and far catchier version of the birthday song.

THE KINGDOM IS NOW
fellow psych tech kicked out of church and that time they asked me to preach for the youth

- *Malkuth* is the Hebrew word for kingdom and refers to the authority and rule of God. Scholars are split. Some believe the term "kingdom of God" refers to the Christian way of living while others maintain that the gospel writers are speaking of the age to come.
- "Notorious sinners are entering the kingdom of God in front of you."—Matthew 21:31 WNT
- "Heal the sick, and tell them, 'The kingdom of God is near you now."—Luke 10:9 NLT
- "Some Pharisees asked Jesus when the kingdom of God would come. His answer was, 'The kingdom of God does not come in such a way as to be seen. No one will say, 'Look, here it is!' or, 'There it is!'; because the kingdom of God is within you.'"—Luke 17:20–21 GNT
- "The Rock that was uncut by human hands, that

destroyed the kingdoms of this world, is even now covering the earth as the waters cover the sea. This is the kingdom that we serve, the kingdom that has come, the kingdom that is forever. This is the one kingdom we all seek."—R. C. Sproul Jr.

· The Bible verse that says the grace I give will be measured back to me the same is Mark 4:24: "With the measure you use, it will be measured to you—and even more" (NIV).

· Jesus warns against obsessing over the speck of sawdust in someone else's eye in Matthew 7:5: "You hypocrite, first take the plank out of your own eye, and then you will see clearly to remove the speck from your brother's eye" (NIV).

· The song that talks about how Christians should be happy all the time is a kids' song called "Inright Outright" or "Happy All the Time," and comes complete with a rousing set of hand motions.

JUMBO THIN MINT AND THE JAUNDICED CHIMP
in which I appear on Christian television

· In Psalm 2:4 it says God sits in the heavens and laughs.

· "Because the foolishness of God is wiser than men."
—1 Corinthians 1:25 ESV

· "I became the laughingstock of all my peoples."
—Lamentations 3:14 NIV

· David danced half-naked in the street in 2 Samuel 6:14–20.

· Ezekiel's bread baking method is described in Ezekiel 4:9–12: "Take wheat and barley, beans and lentils, millet and spelt; put them in a storage jar and use them to make bread for yourself. You are to eat it during the 390 days you lie on your side. Weigh out twenty shekels of food to eat each day and eat it at set times. Also measure out a sixth of a hin of water and drink it at set times. Eat the food as you would a loaf of barley bread; bake it in the sight of the people, using human excrement for fuel."

· John the Baptist ate locusts in Matthew 3:4.

· John the Revelator saw seven-headed dragons in the sky in Revelation 12:3.

THIS IS THE MATTRESS TRICK
where we trick a despondent young psych patient out of his knife

· "Night and day among the tombs and in the hills he would cry out and cut himself with stones"—Mark 5:5 NIV

· "Be kind, for everyone you meet is fighting a hard battle."—John Watson

· Seclusion rooms are often painted soft pink to be calming.

THE EPIPHANY OF THE HOLY AND OF THE ABSURD
the one with all the drums in a single-wide trailer

· King David and crew had a mighty celebration with castanets, harps, tambourines, and cymbals in 2 Samuel 6:5.

· Neil Peart took on the Pharisees on Rush's 2007 release *Snakes & Arrows*.

WALK ON WATER
where I'm a misfit Jesus in the church play and meet a man on the midnight bridge rail

- Isaiah 53:2 features a prophecy of Jesus that pretty much defeats any notion of a good-looking, charming Jesus. "There was nothing beautiful or majestic about his appearance, nothing to attract us to him."

- "He was . . . a man of sorrows and acquainted with grief." —Isaiah 53:3 NASB

- "Truly, O God of Israel, our Savior, you work in mysterious ways."—Isaiah 45:15 NLT

CRAZY, MESSY THINGS
where I get smacked with a chair by Satan and admit a colleague into the psych ward

- Jesus got mad and made a whip in John 2:15: "After making a whip out of cords, he drove all of them out of the Temple, including the sheep and cattle. He scattered the coins of the moneychangers and knocked over their tables" (ISV).

- Jesus asked, "How long do I have to put up with these guys?" in Luke 9:41.

- Jesus said, "My burden is light" in Matthew 11:30.

- The Bible describes Jesus starting his ministry when he was thirty in Luke 3:23.

- "How long do I have to put up with you?"—Luke 9:41 GNT

- "While it was still dark, Jesus . . . went away to a secluded place, and was praying there."—Mark 1:35 NASB

· Schizophrenics often believe themselves to be God or Satan. Some researchers propose that right temporal lobe activity occurs in healthy individuals having a religious experience while right temporal lobe dysfunction is present in schizophrenia.

JUST ONE SIGN
where I consider quitting mental health before meeting a suicidal punk from LA

· Jonah ran from God by heading down to the town of Jaffa (now known as Joppa) and buying a ticket to go on a boat going to Tarshish. "But Jonah got up and went in the opposite direction in order to get away from the LORD." —Jonah 1:3 NLT

· "Everyone, without exception, who calls on the name of the Lord shall be saved."—Romans 10:13 WNT

BAD JAMIE AND THE OLD RUGGED CROSS
that one where they throw me in jail

· "I don't really understand myself, for I want to do what is right, but I don't do it. Instead, I do what I hate." —Romans 7:15 NLT

· "God leads the prisoners out with singing."—Psalm 68:6 NIV

· Jesus is called Wonderful Counselor in Isaiah 9:6.

· The Nietzsche quote Dr. Cryer scribbled on the board: "He who fights monsters should see to it that in the process he does not become a monster."

PICK WONDER
frazzled from a long night on psych, I play pinball and ponder what Jesus was like at twenty-five

- The Bible is largely silent on Jesus' life from ages twelve to thirty.

- The paraphrase of the principle Jesus taught about choosing wonder over worry is taken from a variety of translations of Matthew 6:25–34.

- "But the Lord answered and said to her, 'Martha, Martha, you are worried and bothered about so many things; but only one thing is necessary.'"—Luke 10:41–42 NASB

- "Let heaven fill your thoughts; don't spend your time worrying about things down here."—Colossians 3:2 TLB

- Daniel 10:6 describes a face that flashed like lightning and eyes like lamps of fire.

- *Black Knight* was the first multi-level pinball machine.

TREASURES IN THE DARK
outlaw Bible study in the psych ward courtyard

- The opening quote is from Luke 5:4, where Jesus says, "Push out into deep water, and lower your nets for a catch" (ISV).

- The verse Crazy Mary reads is Psalm 23:2.

- The passage about darkness and the whirlwind comes from Job 38.

- Jesus' warning that those we call lost just might be closer to the kingdom is taken mostly from the parable of the

Pharisee and the tax collector. The good news that says "no matter where you are or how far gone, there is always a way back home" is best illustrated in the parable of the prodigal son. But really, both messages are cover to cover, if you know how to look.

· "For the proud shall be humbled, but the humble shall be honored.'"—Luke 18:9–14 TLB

OF POMP AND CIRCUMSTANCES
the one where I get my master's degree and go straight back to work at the roller rink

· Blood to the bridles of horses (Revelation 14:20).

· Rebel angels having sex with the daughters of men (Genesis 6:4).

· Stuttering, angry Moses, denied the promised land (Numbers 20).

· Lustful, murdering David, a man after God's own heart (2 Samuel 11).

· Solomon's wisdom neutered by concubines (1 Kings 11).

· Ezekiel's wheel of fire in the sky (Ezekiel 1).

· Kamikaze Samson and his suicide mission from on high (Judges 16).

· The prophet Hosea ordered to marry a whore (Hosea 1:2).

· "Make insight your priority."—Proverbs 2:3 THE MESSAGE

· Psalm 18:11 speaks of God shrouding himself in darkness.

· The 1994 Convention of Christian Existentialists lobbied

to get "The Hokey Pokey" included in select midwestern hymnals.

LIKE CHAINSAW JUGGLING OR WRESTLING BEARS
where I get hired at a megachurch counseling center

· The six-wing creatures covered with eyes are described by John in Revelation 4:6–8 while the locust armies swarm through the second chapter of Joel.

· Wild women driving tent stakes through the temples of men: "Then Jael . . . took a tent peg in one hand and a hammer in the other. She crept up on [Sisera], drove the tent peg through his temple into the ground while he was asleep from exhaustion, and he died."—Judges 4:21 NET

· "And when you pray, don't babble on and on like the pagans, who think God will hear them better if they talk a lot."—Matthew 6:7 CJB

· Rabbi Rami Shapiro's exegesis of Ecclesiastes 1:18 says, "The more you do for control, the less you do for joy." Love that.

· You can find a pair of interviews I did with Anne Lamott where we discuss Jesus, The Beatles, and favorite TV preachers at jamieblaine.com.

SUNSHINE SOMEDAY, MAYBE
in which a girl from church begs me to help her friend who works at a strip club

· "If this man really were a prophet, he would know what sort of woman is touching him. She's a sinner."—Luke 7:39 GW

- "By faith Rahab the harlot did not perish."—Hebrews 11:31 NASB
- "Where it's sin versus grace, grace wins hands down." —Romans 5:20 THE MESSAGE
- "Now, y'all without sin can cast the first stone." —H. I. McDunnough
- The fourth man in the fire refers to the story of Shadrach, Meshach, and Abednego in Daniel 3.

BELIEVE THE BEST
where the sorority girl skating party is crashed by orphans

- "No eye has seen, no ear has heard and no one's heart has imagined all the things that God has prepared for those who love him."—1 Corinthians 2:9 CJB
- The verse that says God is sheer mercy and grace is Psalm 103:8 (THE MESSAGE).
- That part in the Bible that says Jesus seeks out and earnestly believes the best about me? Actually, it's Genesis to Revelation. If that's not the message, we're all in trouble.
- The blue merle Australian Shepherd has two different colored eyes and is known for its intuition and loyalty.

JESUS LAUGHS (I HOPE)
the one where I have to go get the drunk girl out of the church thrift store

- The opening quote from Joey Ramone is from Lisa

Robinson's "Rebel Nights," *Vanity Fair*, November 2002, http://www.vanityfair.com/culture/2002/11/new-york-rock-scene-1970s.

- You can find a link to my interview with Lisa as well as one I did with Marky Ramone describing how much Joey and Johnny loved Cracker Barrel at jamieblaine.com.

- Christ walked on water in Matthew 14:22.

- Peter and Paul brought the dead back to life (Acts 9:36–41, Acts 20:7–12).

- Judas stole money and hung himself from the tree (Matthew 27).

- James and John were called twin Sons of Thunder (Mark 3:17).

- Thomas refused to believe until he had seen the nail prints in Jesus' hand (John 20).

- "But You, O LORD, laugh; you scoff at all the nations." —Psalm 59:8 NASB

- "In your presence is fullness of joy."—Psalm 16:11 NKJV

HANDSHAKES AND SIDE HUGS, THAT'S ALL
nice girl from church wants to be friends, maybe more

- "Don't worry about tomorrow. Tomorrow will worry about itself."—Matthew 6:34 CJB

- "For now we see through a glass, darkly."—1 Corinthians 13:12 KJV

- "Everyone is but a breath, even those who seem secure." —Psalm 39:5 NIV

- "The trees of the field shall clap their hands."—Isaiah 55:12 KJV

- King Solomon talks of smoke in the wind and how meaningless everything seems in the entire book of Ecclesiastes.

- Jonah's stumbling is described in the book of Jonah, where he runs from God repeatedly.

- Moses stuttered and stumbled through the desert in Numbers, Exodus, and Deuteronomy. It took him forty years to make an eleven day trip.

ONE OF US
where the homeless guy offers to share his bottle . . .

- The reference to Jesus making room in the kingdom for Skeeter comes from Luke 14:21: "[And the Master said,] 'Quickly, get out into the city streets and alleys. Collect all who look like they need a square meal, all the misfits and homeless and wretched you can lay your hands on, and bring them here'" (THE MESSAGE).

- "But don't forget to be friendly to outsiders; for in so doing, some people, without knowing it, have entertained angels."—Hebrews 13:2 CJB

SAVE A STAR
. . . and another homeless guy offers to share his food

- Jesus says essentially "Where were you when I was sick? When I was in jail? How about when I was hungry? Where were you when I lost my mind?" in Matthew 25.

- Our solar system is a mere speck within the Milky Way galaxy. The nearest spiral galaxy to ours is Andromeda, 2.5 million light-years away. The Hubble Deep Field image suggests that the observable universe contains approximately 200 billion galaxies.

- "For one star differs from another star in glory."
—1 Corinthians 15:41 NKJV

- Enoch is taken up by God in Genesis 5:24.

- Falling stars are actually meteors as they enter Earth's atmosphere and burn.

- "The heavens declare the glory of God."—Psalm 19:1 ESV

STANDING ON THE HILLTOP WITH BOTH HANDS IN THE AIR

I go to the sermon series on finding purpose and ride in the assistant pastor's El Camino

- "But seek first his kingdom and his righteousness, and all these things will be given to you as well."—Matthew 6:33 CJB

- "For man looks on the outward appearance, but the LORD looks on the the heart."—I Samuel 16:7 ESV

- "Much learning earns you much trouble."—Ecclesiastes 1:18 THE MESSAGE

- "The Hebrew text is beautifully unruly, often ambiguous, multiple in meaning and hard to pin down; many of the English translations are, above all, certain."—Aviya Kushner

- Anxiety is the fruit of unbalanced teaching on purpose and plans.

· "Don't Try So Hard" is a song from Amy Grant's *How Mercy Looks From Here*. Amy and I had a great conversation about misfits, radical kindness, and how to sneak a guitar into services at the Church of Christ. Find it at jamieblaine.com.

BLACK BELT BIBLE MONSTERS
in which my tattooed hairdresser tells me about her Jesus dream

· "Be merciful to those who doubt."—Jude 1:22 NIV

· "Be quick to listen, slow to speak."—James 1:19 NIV

· Psalm 9:9 says that the Lord is a refuge to the humble and a shelter in troubling times.

· "For you are my hiding place."—Psalm 32:7 NLT

· In Matthew 6:6 Jesus says we should go to a secret place, shut the door, and pray to God in private.

CHRISTMAS CRAZY AT THE DOLLAR GENERAL STORE
struggling to find the spirit of Christmas, I stumble across a teenage mother and child

· Suddenly, an angel stood among them and God's glory blazed all around. And the angel said, "Don't be afraid. I'm here to announce a great and joyful event that is meant for everybody, worldwide: A Savior has just been born in Bethlehem. This is what you're to look for: a baby wrapped in a blanket and lying in a trough."—Luke 2:9–12 THE MESSAGE

- The secret to perfect fountain coke lies in the mixture of co2.
- God did call a truce. That's what Christmas is.

DRIVE ON
grace for all and a wreck in the rain

- Jesus chooses Peter—of all people—to build his church upon, in Matthew 16:18.
- The thief pleads, "Remember me," to Jesus on the cross in Luke 23:42.
- "Beware the leaven of the Pharisees."—Luke 12:1 ESV
- "Everything they do is for show."—Matthew 23:5 NLT
- "Confess your faults one to another, and pray."—James 5:16 KJV
- "Wisdom is the principal thing."—Proverbs 4:7 KJV

THANKS FOR THE PUSH
where I fail miserably trying to impress the girl from church

- Pondering dibs on serendipity is a reference to Job 1:6–7. "One day the angels came to report to God and Satan tagged along. God singled him out and said, 'And what have you been up to?'"
- "Many are the plans in a person's heart, but it is the LORD's purpose that prevails."—Proverbs 19:21 NIV
- "In peace I will lie down and sleep, for you alone, LORD, make me dwell in safety."—Psalm 4:8 NIV

PRETTY DANG SWEET

in which a scruffy little six-year-old kid asks me to skate

- "Carry each other."—Galatians 6:2 NIV
- "And a little child shall lead them all."—Isaiah 11:6 NLT

BETTER THAN ZAXXON

where a man on his death bed teaches me something about life

- "I'm telling you a mystery: Not all of us will die, but we will all be changed."—1 Corinthians 15:51 GW
- "And the last enemy to be destroyed is death." —1 Corinthians 15:26 NLT

LET GO OF THE ROPES AND FADE AWAY

in which I buy decent clothes for a job with the state

- "Can all your worries add one single moment to your life?"—Matthew 6:27 NLT
- The Bible speaks of going from glory to glory in 2 Corinthians 3:18.
- The devotion I read that spoke of living light and learning to walk in the unforced rhythms of grace was from *The Message*'s translation of Matthew 11:28–30.
- "Our passionate preoccupation with the sky, the stars, and a God somewhere in outer space is a homing impulse. We are drawn back to where we came from."—Eric Hoffer
- "He made the moon and stars to rule the night. His love continues forever."—Psalm 136:9 NCV

777: FAVOR
late night pinball and Brooke's return

· In Hebrew tradition, seven is considered to be the number of perfection. 777 is sometimes believed to symbolize the threefold perfection of the Holy Trinity.

· "Seventy 'sevens' are decreed for your people and your holy city to finish transgression, to put an end to sin, to atone for wickedness, to bring in everlasting righteousness, to seal up vision and prophecy and anoint the Most Holy Place."—Daniel 9:24 NIV

· The Bible says that God has my name engraved on his hand in Isaiah 49:16.

· "Live creatively, friends."—Galatians 6:1 THE MESSAGE

· "And when two or three of you are together because of me, you can be sure that I'll be there."—Matthew 18:20 THE MESSAGE

WHEREVER YOU ARE TONIGHT
sweet church service from the balcony

· Strangers in a strange land is a reference from Exodus 2:22.

· "Finally, all of you should be of one mind, full of sympathy toward each other, loving one another with tender hearts and humble minds."—1 Peter 3:8 NLT

· "Save us, Oh God, for the waters rise" is taken from Psalm 69.

· "The wreck of your hands" is a rumination on Genesis

6:6 where God regrets having made man and all the Psalms where King David is so brutally honest about his wrecked-ness.

· "Here's what I've decided is the best way to live: Take care of yourself, have a good time, and make the most of whatever job you have for as long as God gives you life. And that's about it. That's the human lot."—Ecclesiastes 5:18 THE MESSAGE

· In Matthew 28:20 Jesus says he is with us always, even to the end of the age.

· 2 Corinthians 5:1 says there is no end.

JUST KEEP WALKING

maybe every ending is only a beginning again

· "Walk with me . . . learn the unforced rhythms of grace."—Matthew 11:28 THE MESSAGE

· "I will give you the treasures of darkness and hidden wealth of secret places, so that you may know that it is I, The LORD . . . who calls you by name."—Isaiah 45:3 NASB

· "The deep covered me completely."—Jonah 2:5 GW

ABOUT THE AUTHOR

JAMIE BLAINE IS A LICENSED PSYCHOTHERAPIST AND journalist who has worked in megachurches, mental hospitals, libraries, haunted houses, rehabs, radio stations, and roller rinks across the South. He is music editor of the *Salon* affiliate *The Weeklings*, nonfiction editor of the LA literary collective *The Nervous Breakdown*, and his writing has been featured in publications such as *Drummer UK, Bass Guitar, Music Industry News, Salon, Acoustic Guitar, Ultimate Classic Rock, The Contributor, OnFaith,* and *The Wittenburg Door.* Blaine lives in Nashville, Tennessee.